all in
finding true life on the path to total surrender

mike guzzardo

MOODY PUBLISHERS
CHICAGO

Published in association with literary agent Jenni Burke of D.C. Jacobson & Associates, an Author Management Company, www.DCJacobson.com.

Edited by Christopher Reese
Interior design: Ragont Design   Cover design: Left Coast Design

Library of Congress Cataloging-in-Publication Data
Guzzardo, Mike.
    All in : finding true life on the path to total surrender / Mike Guzzardo.
       p. cm.
    Includes bibliographical references.
    ISBN 978-0-8024-1783-1
    1. Submissiveness—Religious aspects—Christianity. 2. Will—Religious aspects—Christianity. 3. Spirituality. I. Title.
    BV4647.A25G89 2010
    248.4--dc22
                                                                2011012535

Also available as an EBook 978-0-8024-7809-2

We hope you enjoy this book from Moody Publishers. Our goal is to provide high-quality, thought-provoking books and products that connect truth to your real needs and challenges. For more information on other books and products written and produced from a biblical perspective, go to www.moodypublishers. com or write to:

Moody Publishers
820 N. LaSalle Boulevard
Chicago, IL 60610

3 5 7 9 10 8 6 4 2

Printed in the United States of America

contents

foreword

I met Mike Guzzardo more than ten years ago when we asked him to join our staff after seeing him successfully lead several of our international trips. From the beginning, Mike's life has been marked by his focus on and passion for the deep truths of God—which he pursues relentlessly. He will never settle for a life that falls short of completing the mission God has given him. He pores through the Bible, sermons, and other books regularly for a greater understanding of God's truth. There is nothing more important to Mike in life than God's truth (but his wife and daughter come in at a close second)!

Now, after having spoken to hundreds of thousands of teenagers at Acquire the Fire youth events, Mike's heart for young people is without question and his impact on them is written on the fabric of their lives.

Throughout our travels together across the United States
and around the world, Mike and I have both noticed the rapid
decline of absolute truth in the beliefs of young people today.
My heart breaks to see how culture and media often become
our first love in place of the true adventure of following Christ.
Mike and I have both been affected by the people we
encounter. They cry on our shoulders and recount how hearing God's truth brought them freedom. They are looking for
a strong faith. One that would give them the courage to break
free from the only life they know. One that would fill their
desire to matter, to make a difference—which in reality is each
person's desire to worship their Savior.

Mike wrote this book for the thousands of young people
wondering if there is any meaning to life outside the parties,
media fads, and a church life void of passion. Read it. Think
about it. Live it.

Ron Luce
President, Teen Mania Ministries

introduction

This book is for the thousands of people I have spoken with during my travels who are not experiencing God the way they desire. It's not that they haven't experienced God at all— it's that their level of experience with God to this point has been below what they hoped. They've heard that an amazing, life-transforming walk with God is possible, but their own spiritual reality seems to fall short. They are trying to remain positive while battling the notion that says, "I guess this is all there is."

God promises that it does not have to be this way.

Deep down, we all want to experience more of God. We just aren't sure how to get there. In our disappointment we wonder if there is some secret information we've missed. Surprising as it may seem, many of you reading these words may already posses the *knowledge* necessary for a deeper experience with God. While it is true there may be some gaps in our understanding of how to live our lives in a way that leads to a radical experience with God, our problem most often lies not in our lack of *information*, but in our lack of *application*. Could it be that the answer we seek is something that we already *know* deep in our hearts but simply have never *put into practice*?

James 1:22 says, "But don't just listen to God's word. You must do what it says. Otherwise, you are only fooling yourselves" (NLT). This verse reminds us that it will not help us to merely know something—we must do it.

H. Richard Niebuhr said, "The great Christian revolutions come not by the discovery of something that was not known before. They happen when somebody takes radically something that was always there."[1] I believe this principle is not just true of corporate revolutions but private, individual revolutions as well.

Believe it or not, the kind of walk with God you have always hoped for may not be as far off as you thought. Anyone who is willing to put into practice the principles Jesus outlined for us *will* experience Him in a life-transforming way.

As you read this book, resist the temptation to simply read for information. The answer to your search will be found not in your answer to the question, "Do I *understand* this?", but rather in your answer to the question, "Am I *applying* this principle to my life?" This is always how your greatest life transformation will be found. Remember, truth that is known but not applied will never change you. (This is revelation without application.)

As we discuss what it looks like to live the kind of life that Jesus promises will lead to the kind of experience with Him that we all desire, undoubtedly you will find hindrances and roadblocks in your heart and mind that make walking in or applying His instructions difficult. In fact, we will discuss what I believe to be the Enemy's main weapon that has derailed many from walking in the kind of surrender to which Jesus calls us. As you identify and remove this weapon, many of the roadblocks that hindered your ability to live a life of surrender will fall away, thus paving the way for you to have an experience with God that goes beyond what you thought possible.

To assist you, the following chapters include many Scriptures you can meditate on and memorize. The Word of God is living and active. It has supernatural power to transform you. As you read, highlight any Scriptures you feel are helpful so that you can refer back to them on your journey.

If you ever feel that there must be more to Christianity than what you are experiencing, this book is for you. If you ever wonder why your life looks the same year after year after year, this book is for you. If you ever long to finally rid yourself of certain sins and follow God with all your heart, this book is for you. If you ever feel like there is a great gulf between the life you have and the life you want in Christ, this book is for you. My sincere prayer is that your hope will be reignited about what is possible in your relationship with God.

It *IS* possible to experience more of God. Let's find out together how to go all in.

chapter 1

camping out or climbing?

Have you ever thought about following Jesus the same way you think about climbing a mountain? **Think of it as ascending a mountain of spiritual progress where with each step Jesus leads us up the mountain higher and higher into the overcoming life He desires for us.**

The analogy might go something like this: Jesus asks us to come and follow Him so He can lead us to the abundant life we all so desperately desire. If we say yes to His call, we meet Him at the bottom of the mountain to begin our journey. However, we each show up with a heavy backpack filled with a lifetime of fears, sins, insecurities, addictions, comforts, and other hindrances we have accumulated. Although Jesus knows our heavy packs will make it hard to climb, He is a patient guide, so in His love He looks at us with our huge backpacks and simply says, "Okay—let's go!" So our journey begins.

God's goal is always for us to reach the pinnacle of the mountain—a life of freedom, abundance, and the fulfillment of our God-given destiny. Every step we take with Him brings us higher up the mountain. The higher up we get, the more we experience God and see His promises coming to pass in our lives.

As we journey on with the Lord, there will be times when we come to places where we can't manage to climb over a rock or squeeze through a crevice. We are unable to continue. At each place like this, we discover that something must be removed from our heavy backpack if we want to continue on with Him. As our guide, Jesus will reveal to us exactly what we must part with in order to move forward. If we choose to lay that thing down, we continue on, climbing beside our Guide, our experience growing with each step as we draw ever closer to the peak.

> **Like a starving man trying to ignore the pains of hunger, something in our hearts persistently aches for more.**

However, if we say "No" and are unwilling to remove something from our pack, our progress stalls. In His love, Jesus doesn't give up on us. He simply takes us back around the mountain and gives us the same test again. It could be days, weeks, or maybe even years later. But the time will come when He asks us again to remove the hindrance from our backpack. Whether we move on depends on our decision in that moment. Will we be willing? Or will our resistance mean that our progress up the mountain stops?

When we cling to our heavy burdens and refuse God's repeated attempts to free us from them, it's almost as if we set up camp on the mountain of spiritual progress, unwilling to do what is necessary to continue. The longer we stay in camp, the more likely we are to believe that this must be all there is. We look at the others camped out all around us and reassure ourselves that surely this must be normal Christianity. "Besides," we reason, "we have made *some* progress—after all, the view here is better than it was at the foot of the mountain."

Yet all the while, far above our camp, the pinnacle still awaits—the abundant life and calling for which God set us apart from the beginning of time. Like a starving man trying to ignore the pains of hunger, something in our hearts persistently aches for more. And Jesus, our Guide, is eager to lead us there—gently nudging us to trust Him and keep climbing.

However, if we choose to say "Yes" each time God asks us to remove something from our backpack, we will continue on. Though at times it may be painful and hard to remove certain things from our pack, it is the only way to leave camp and continue toward the top of the mountain. The further we journey with Him, the more freedom we experience and the more knowledge of God's character we gain.

Over time our lives become the evidence that Jesus is a faithful Guide. Each act of obedience, though at times painful, proves to be a small price when compared to the joy and transformation it produced. The higher we climb, the more we experience the incomparable fulfillment that comes from God's plan unfolding in our lives. We are no longer the same person who began the journey. We are being transformed and set free every day to live the life we always hoped for and scarcely dared dream was possible.

Transformed?

Sadly, this picture of pressing on toward the peak doesn't characterize many who call themselves Christians today. Most Christians seem quite content to camp out on the lower slopes of the mountain, only experiencing a fraction of God's goodness and transforming power.

As I travel across the country to minister, I see the same pattern repeated everywhere. While I always meet some who are clearly following God with all their heart and experiencing Him in a life-changing way, the vast majority seem to be falling far short of the life God intends for them. Because this lack of experience has become the norm, most don't even realize something's missing.

God desires to completely transform *every* part of our lives with His love and power.

But when we reflect on the depth of transformation the Bible promises, our lack becomes evident. For instance,

Hebrews 12:29 says, "our 'God is a consuming fire'." Take a second to think about this analogy. When something is consumed by fire, a complete and total transformation takes place. Take a piece of wood, for example. Before fire consumes it, it is, well, a piece of wood. However, *after* fire consumes it, nothing about that wood is the same anymore. It looks different. It feels different. It has been completely and entirely transformed.

God has given us this analogy—and many others—to help us understand the kind of transformation He wants to accomplish in our lives. He doesn't want to just *mildly* change us or *sort of* change us. God desires to completely transform *every* part of our lives with His love and power. Where we need healing, He wants to heal us. When we need joy, He wants to give us joy. Where we need character, He wants to teach us character.

God wants to transform us until we are completely whole and equipped to live the life He has planned for us. As Paul says in 2 Corinthians 5:17, "Anyone who belongs to Christ has become a new person. The old life is gone; a new life has begun!" (NLT).

Consider the early church. Not long after Jesus was raised from the dead, the term "Christian" was first used to describe those who followed Jesus. Today, this term is something we call ourselves to identify that we believe in Jesus. But when the term began, it wasn't something the people following Jesus decided to call themselves—*other people*, outside the church, gave them that name. These early Christians began looking so much like Jesus—they were so completely transformed—that people said, "You must be a Christ-follower." So they called them "Christians."

Notice that believers in the early church didn't have to label themselves for people to know they were following Christ. Instead, their identity was evident to all by the transformation in their lives and actions.

When I look around today, this kind of experience with God seems to be quite rare. In fact, a recent study by the Barna Group reported that most people who define themselves as Christians are only mildly affected by their faith.[1] Many people believe Jesus is real and may have even prayed a prayer inviting Jesus to "come into" their lives. But in their everyday life, there is little evidence of transformation. For some reason their experience falls far short of the Bible's description of what a life transformed by God will look like.

Quit or Settle?

While the extent of our transformation cannot change God's love for us, it will impact the way we experience Him for the rest of our lives. When we camp on the lower slopes of the mountain, one of two things usually happens—and neither is desirable.

The first outcome is that we quit following Jesus. One study concluded that nearly nine out of ten young people raised in Christian homes will fall away by the time they graduate high school.[2] This is a staggering statistic, but it just proves how dangerous a halfhearted experience with God can be.

The process often looks something like this. People hear the message of the gospel, and the Holy Spirit works in their hearts to draw them to Christ. They come to Jesus with great hopes and a genuine excitement to experience the transformation He brings. However, for reasons we will discuss in the following chapters, they never really experience much transformation in their lives. Over time, they become disinterested in their walk with God because nothing seems to be happening. They may hang on for a while, but pretty soon they conclude that this "Jesus thing" must not be as real as they thought it was. Eventually they abandon their pursuit of Christ altogether.

However, many more Christians fall into the second category. They never leave the church or turn their backs on God. Instead, they settle. Everything continues to look the same. They still agree with the sermons; they may even pray and read the Bible now and again. But they have stopped believing that God can truly transform their lives. Year in and year out they go through the motions, trying to be content with the few fading encounters they have with God. While they may never admit it, deep down they have lost hope that their lives can be transformed and made whole the way God promises.

It's not that they don't believe it's possible—they simply stop believing it's possible for *them*.

Abundant Life

What in the world is going on? Is this really all we can expect in our experience with God?

Thankfully, the answer is no! The Bible is clear that if we choose to follow Jesus, He will lead us to an abundant life of joy and fulfillment. It almost sounds too good to be true, but God confirms this promise over and over again in His Word.

Jesus did not give His life

so we could have an average

experience with Him.

In John 10:10, Jesus says, "The thief does not come except to steal, and to kill, and to destroy. I have come that they may have life, and that they may have it more abundantly" (NKJV). God promises us that He has come to give us an abundant life. The word *abundant* means over and above, more than necessary, excessive, superior, extraordinary, surpassing, and uncommon.[3] Now that's transformation!

Jesus did not give His life so we could have an average experience with Him. He made it possible when we follow Him for us to experience His goodness and transformation in a way that will leave us speechless with gratitude. Yes, it will require sacrifice and surrender, but the results will be worth it many times over.

Are You Ready for the Climb?

Regardless of what your experience with God has been to this point, would you be willing to open your heart to the possibility that you really can experience a life of overwhelming transformation through Christ? Perhaps that is your first step—simply making the choice to believe that God really does have more for you.

So many times past failures or fear of being disappointed cause us to settle for what we know instead of attempting to press onward. The Enemy whispers in our ear, urging us to settle into camp or even trudge back down the mountain.

But God has greater things for you; He'll never leave your side. Wherever you are on the mountain of faith, Jesus is calling you higher. Are you willing to break camp today and press on toward the pinnacle?

I believe this book is not in your hands by accident. God, in His great love for you, wants you to know that He is trustworthy and that He longs to lead you to fullness of life.

If your heart longs for more of God, then the following pages are for you. Together, we will discover what God's offer of abundant life means, why we often fall short of God's intentions for us, and how we can follow Jesus to the top of the mountain where our lives will be transformed. Let's begin by taking a closer look at some specific examples of this abundant life that's promised in order to more clearly understand the "transformation" described in God's Word.

Questions

1. On a scale of 1 to 10, with 1 being no experience and 10 being off the charts, how would you describe your level of experience with God? What made you choose that number? Has that number changed over the years?

2. Right now, is your relationship with God affecting your life as much as you think it should?

3. Where are you on the mountain of spiritual progress? Are you hiking upward? What have you been asked to take out of your backpack? Are you camped out somewhere or walking back down? How did you get to this place?

4. Are you ready to do what it takes to experience more of God and transform your life? Why or why not?

chapter 2

experiencing God's promises

I want to be specific about the transformed and abundant life God has for us. Without looking at the kind of life God desires for us, we can be fooled into believing that whatever we have experienced with God *so far* is all there is—when in fact there are mountain peaks of greater experience still waiting for us. Often, we can be living far below God's best for us and not even know it!

In this chapter, we'll look at a few of the promises that God makes to us in His Word—promises of blessings that can be ours when we follow Him. After each section, I will ask you to compare your own experience with what God has made available. Have you experienced God in this way? Or are you still camping far down the mountain? If you realize you have not yet experienced some of these promises, allow them to give you a view of the mountaintop, and to inspire you to leave camp and follow Jesus' lead.

Deep down we are all crying out to be loved and accepted.

Love

One of the things the Bible promises us is love. No matter what our age, it seems we humans never outgrow our need for love. However, when we are young and forming our identity, the need for love seems to be even more apparent. For example, people gravitate toward different cliques and fads, hoping to fit in. This happens because deep down we are all crying out to be loved and accepted.

For example, have you ever observed what I call an "extreme summer makeover"? This is where in one summer, a guy (or girl) can change his style, his clothes, his friends—his whole identity, all in hopes of gaining acceptance. When you last see him before school lets out for summer he is . . . well let's just call him "preppy guy." You know the type—dresses up for school, always gets amazing grades, proud member of the chess club, etc. But by the time you see him on the first day of school the next year he has completely transformed into . . . "gangsta guy." He dresses with baggy clothes, talks differently, listens to new music, and even tries to walk down the hall with a limp. I'm sure you've seen this process (or something like it) play out multiple times.

While it may not always be as drastic as an "extreme summer makeover," this sort of thing happens all the time: girls dress immodestly to get attention, guys show off for approval, and everyone gossips to validate themselves. The list goes on and on. In some form or fashion *we've all tried to fit in* because deep down we are all desperate for unconditional love and acceptance, like an oxygen-deprived person frantic for air.

This sounds like a hopeless cycle—but there is good news! Zephaniah 3:17 says, "The Lord your God is with you, he is mighty to save. He will take great delight in you, he will quiet you with his love, he will rejoice over you with singing." Consider the picture Zephaniah paints for us: "He will *quiet* you with HIS love."

When we look past people's attempts to fit in, we find hearts that are crying out to be loved. This verse gives us the picture of a love so strong it can literally quiet that cry in our hearts to be loved and accepted. This doesn't mean we won't desire love from other people anymore. After all, God made us to desire relationships with others. But often the Enemy is able to pervert this desire until we feel a yearning for love and acceptance that goes far beyond what is healthy. When this happens, we find ourselves constantly changing our identities, altering our interests, and compromising our morals in an effort to attain the love and approval we crave. Our soul has developed an unhealthy desperation and is literally crying out to be loved at almost any cost.

In reality, the love of others—and especially the fickle social acceptance of others—will never fully satisfy the depth of our desire for love. This deep cry inside of us can only be quieted by the God who created us to need His perfect love. God wants to envelop us with a love so strong it will calm our unhealthy desperation and our feelings of insecurity. When we experience God's love, it brings us to a place of health and security in which we know that we are loved perfectly by the One who matters most. Then we will be free to enjoy the love and acceptance of others from a place of freedom and security instead of desperation and sin.

Now let me ask you the million-dollar question and please don't just breeze over it—*Is God's love having this deep of an impact on your life?* Can you even imagine what it would be like to experience the love of God so deeply that the insecure longings of your heart are quieted? Or are you still seeking the acceptance of others to meet your need for love? Because this is the kind of transformation God is willing and ready to bring into our lives if we will allow Him.

Satisfaction

So many of us live in a constant state of dissatisfaction. We want this and we want that and we think each new thing will make us happy.

But it doesn't.

The deception usually goes something like this: *I would be content if I could just have (fill in the blank).* We all know the drill. *If I could just look a little more like the model on the magazine, or be a little more popular, or have that certain girlfriend, guitar, grade, or sports position.* We then live in a state of dissatisfaction until we get that one magical thing.

The problem is, it's a no-win situation. If we *don't* get what we want, we are dissatisfied because we don't have it. But even if we *do* get what we want, the excitement wears off after a few weeks, days, or even hours. We then find something new to fill in that blank, and the whole exhausting process starts all over again. If we're not careful, we will waste much of our lives on this hamster wheel, running hard after satisfaction, but never making any progress.

In Psalm 63, David is talking about His relationship with God and spending time in His presence. In the first part of verse 5, David says that when he is in God's presence, "My soul will be satisfied as with the richest of foods." David learned that as he spent time with God, this relationship brought satisfaction and contentment to his life. And remember, King David could have had *anything* he wanted to keep him happy.

When we feel discontent, it is so easy to run toward television, food, shopping, video games, social events, and vacations. We look to these things to fill the void instead of finding permanent satisfaction in God like David did. He tried everything the world offered to make him content, yet he concluded that the only way to be *truly* happy for a lifetime was to experience God.

The truth is, the greatest satisfaction we will ever feel is from doing the will of God. When we do the will of God, we are lining up our lives with the purpose for which we were created. Living in line with our true purpose will always keep us on a path of deep fulfillment.

Think about a microwave oven. This invention was created with one purpose in mind, to quickly heat food. While you can choose to use a microwave to store extra papers or house your hamster, it will always produce the best results when it's doing what it was created to do—heat food. In the same way, your life will always produce the highest level of satisfaction when you live in line with the purpose God designed you for.

The more we experience God's true satisfaction, the more our desire for counterfeit alternatives will fade away.

When we feel a continual sense of discontentment, frustration, or dissatisfaction, these are like warning flares shooting up from the depths of our soul revealing that somewhere our lives have gotten out of sync with God's plan. What we should do in those moments is go to the Lord and allow Him to show us where we have veered off course and then readjust our lives. When we do this, we reengage with the path of satisfaction. However, instead of running to the Lord when discontentment arises, we too often run to a food or a hobby or the television. The problem is, these things have absolutely no power to restore our contentment. They simply serve as a temporary distraction causing us to ignore the warning signals of our soul and deprive it of the cure for its condition. The longer we persist in running to these inadequate remedies, the further we veer from God's plan and the more true contentment eludes us.

When we feel discontent, we must learn to ask God to help us identify the cause and then follow His directions instead of running to a temporary pacifier. The more we experience

God's true satisfaction, the more our desire for counterfeit alternatives will fade away.

Have you experienced the kind of enduring satisfaction that comes from consistently walking in step with Jesus? Or does that level of contentment seem like an unattainable dream? This kind of contentment really is available to you. If it seems a far cry from your reality, let it serve to awaken you to the truth that greater heights in God await you!

The truth is that God has made freedom available to us in every area that holds us captive.

More than likely, the degree to which you have experienced God's enduring satisfaction will be determined by your answer to the question, "When I am faced with feelings of discontentment, frustration, and dissatisfaction, where do I turn? Do I turn to God or do I turn to (fill in the blank)?"

Freedom

Freedom is another promise God makes available to us. Jesus says in John 8:36, "So if the Son sets you free, you will be free indeed." Often when we are wrestling with issues of sin in our lives, we are confused when we look at a verse like this. If God has set us free from the power of sin, why do so many of us feel like we're still slaves?

The truth is that God has made freedom available to us in every area that holds us captive.

When we notice an area of our lives in which we are continually sinning, it doesn't mean that freedom is impossible. It simply reveals an area where Satan has tricked us into believing that sin will successfully meet a need or fill a void in our lives. As long as we allow that deception to remain, our lives seem hopelessly drawn to that sin like metal to a magnet.

For example, I have seen many girls wounded by not getting the love and affection they needed from their fathers. Satan then takes advantage of their situation and cons them into believing that attention from another man can fill their void. This erroneous belief leads them to consistently give their hearts and bodies away, bringing great destruction to their lives. Unless this lie is exposed, they will continue to live in slavery to this sin.

However, once this deception is removed, and they are able to understand that this kind of behavior cannot bring healing—and in fact will only continue to harm them—the desire for this sin will fade away. Without that magnet of desire constantly pulling on them, they become completely free. The same process is true with any sin.

John 16:13 reminds us that Jesus promised to send us the Holy Spirit to guide us into all truth. This means that as we spend time in God's Word and yield to the leading of the Holy Spirit, He will give us the necessary truth to overcome every deception in our mind. The more we allow Jesus' truth to change our thinking, the freer we will become.

This process of God helping us remove the deceptions that cause us to sin and then leading us to freedom is something that God has made available to all of us and should be a normal part of our Christian walk. While it is true that in some areas gaining freedom can be a lengthy process, we should be able to look back and identify many areas in which we were once slaves but are now experiencing freedom in Christ.

What has been your personal experience with the freedom God brings? Do you feel free? Or do you at least feel like you are making progress towards greater freedom? Can you look at your life and see areas where you have struggled with sin in the past and attained victory? Or do you feel like you're sinning more now than ever? Is freedom something you *continually* experience in your walk with the Lord, or is it only an occasional reality?

Joy isn't just a feeling— it's a choice!

If freedom seems hard to come by in your life right now, don't be discouraged! The good news is that complete freedom really is available to you in Christ. Remember that the purpose of reviewing these promises is to help you realize that there is more of God and His amazing life available to you. The more we realize just how much we are missing, the more motivated we become to break camp and press on.

Joy

The Bible promises us an enduring joy that we can experience through the ups and downs of life. Psalm 16:11 says,

"You will show me the path of life; in Your presence is fullness of joy; at Your right hand are pleasures forevermore" (NKJV). Can you even imagine what *fullness of joy* in your life would look like? Does that sound too good to be true? It isn't. The truth is, joy is not just an emotion we feel when things are going well. That is better described as happiness. We tend to mistake happiness for joy. Happiness depends on our circumstances. Joy, on the other hand, is independent of our circumstances.

Galatians 5:22 tells us that joy is a fruit of God's Spirit. Because joy comes from God, only He, not circumstances, can give it. Because He has already chosen to make His joy available to us, it is actually something we can experience at all times. Believe it or not, joy isn't just a feeling—it's a choice!

That is why the Bible can instruct us to rejoice always (Philippians 4:4). If joy were simply an emotion that was dependent on how well our day went, this command would make no sense. Our joy level will always follow our perspective. If we choose to dwell on all the bad things going on in our life, it won't matter how many good things there are—we will have little joy. However, if we continue to focus on what God has given us, even in the midst of hard times, we will experience His joy.

This is why Psalm 16:11 can say that fullness of joy is found in God's presence. As we spend time in God's presence and submit to His leadership, God will transform our perspective. He will change our understanding of what is important in this life and in eternity. The unimportant things of this life will no longer steal our joy. When God transforms our perspective, we begin to see life differently, and fullness of joy becomes a reality for us—even when our circumstances are bad.

For example, in Acts 5:40–41 we see the disciples were able to rejoice even after they had been whipped and jailed for their faith! Why? Well, Jesus had told them that when they were persecuted for their faith their reward would be great (Matthew 5:11–12). So even in the midst of terrible circumstances, the disciples were able to experience joy because they chose to allow God's truth to shape their perspective. When we allow God to shape our perspective, He will do the same for us.

What about you? Do you experience joy like the disciples in your walk with God? Despite normal moments of heartache and difficulty, is there a resounding joy in your heart? Or do you feel a lack of joy day in and day out? Perhaps you have even struggled with suicidal thoughts or depression.[1]

Even when everything in life is falling apart, God is still able to give you peace.

Does true joy seem like a myth? Do you believe you can ever experience the fullness of God's joy? As incredible as it may seem, this is just another example of the fullness of life God wants you to experience.

Peace

With all the ups and downs of life, peace can seem hard to come by at times. Yet in Philippians 4:7, Paul writes that "the peace of God, which surpasses all understanding, will guard your hearts and minds through Christ Jesus" (NKJV). This verse tells us that there is a peace available to us through Christ that is so strong it "surpasses all understanding"!

Can you imagine a peace so powerful that you experience it even when the circumstances of life are the opposite of peaceful? Even when everything in life is falling apart, God is still able to give you peace. When life seems unbearable, God can provide peace that will guard our hearts and minds from the fear and anxiety that threaten to overwhelm us. Think about Paul and his companions singing praise songs while in prison (Acts 16:24–25). Clearly, their peace was not dependent on their circumstances! This is the kind of peace only God can give.

I experienced this truth firsthand when God called me to leave my job and begin speaking full time. When I first heard His call, I had a very secure job and had just gotten into a serious relationship with the girl who would later become my wife. As God's call to speak grew stronger and stronger in my heart, I knew I had to obey. I was very nervous about trading a secure job for a life of trusting God for provision. What if no one wanted me to speak? To make matters worse, the month I finally quit my job was the same month I got married!

Deep in my heart I knew this was what God wanted for us and that it wasn't His desire that I feel such anxiety. After all, His Word is *full* of promises that He will provide for our needs. I realized I needed to alter my perspective so that I could walk in the peace God had already made available to all

His children. I began to fight my fear by spending time in God's presence, pouring out my heart to Him in prayer, and meditating on His promises of provision.

After a few weeks, I saw a complete transformation in the way I was feeling. My circumstances hadn't changed—it still didn't *seem* like I would have enough money—but God gave me a peace that surpassed understanding. He gave me a confidence that I could trust the promises in His Word. Looking back, I am amazed by the creative ways God provided for us during that time. But perhaps the greatest miracle was the peace God gave me.

Take a second to evaluate the level of peace in your life. Do you consistently experience a peace that surpasses all understanding? Or does that sound completely foreign to you? Do you find your peace being swallowed by worry throughout the day?

Perhaps *peaceful* is the last word you would use to describe your life. If your life is lacking peace, be encouraged: True peace really is available to you! Can you imagine living a life in which God transforms your perspective and provides you with lasting peace?

What's the Deal?

The Bible clearly says that we should be experiencing love, satisfaction, freedom, joy, peace, and countless other good promises of God's abundant life. When our lives look different from those promises, we may find ourselves asking, *What's the problem? Why am I falling short? Is Jesus still there? Is God's Word no longer relevant? Why aren't I experiencing what God promised?!*

The simple truth is that God's promises are as real today as they have ever been—God is the same yesterday, today, and forever. The problem is not with God or the promises in His Word.

The problem is us.

In short, we don't experience very much of God and His promises because we have chosen to settle—content to remain in camp far down the mountain. But we don't have to stay there! God is bursting at the seams to lead us onward so we can experience His abundant life to the full. I hope the previous pages have awakened a hunger in your heart by giving you a glimpse of what could be. Would you be willing to take a step of faith, laying aside your chains of fear to completely trust your life to Jesus' guidance? This is all that is necessary to move on! Yes, it will take commitment and yes, there will be times when following Jesus' instructions will seem difficult —but what's the alternative? Continuing to settle for a mediocre experience with God and a life that never really takes hold of true joy, peace, and fulfillment?

God has extended His hand as an invitation to lead you to a full life. And I know deep in your heart you long for more of God and the life He brings. If you will allow yourself to receive the truth that *it really is possible for you*, desire will again well up in your heart, urging you to respond. And this simple response of the heart—turning your back on comfort, complacency, and familiarity to grab His outstretched hand— is how your journey begins.

Questions

1. How does reading about the amazing promises in this chapter make you feel?

2. Which promise stood out to you the most, and why?

3. How does your experience compare with what God makes available to each of us?

4. Do you feel like you are moving forward in these areas, or backward? Or both?

5. Do you honestly believe that you can experience the fullness of these and other promises that God speaks of in His Word?

chapter 3

nothing
held back

In June of 1998, I was preparing to go on a summer mission trip to Botswana, Africa. Since I was going as a leader, I asked the Lord what messages He wanted me to share with the teenagers throughout the summer. As I prayed, the Lord spoke clearly to my heart: "Mike, the greatest problem with the church in America today is that everyone is looking at a relationship with Me as an addition to their lives."

Does this sound familiar? It's as if we come to God thinking, *I've got tons of priorities in my life. I've got my job, my friends, my hobbies, my boyfriend or girlfriend . . . may as well throw Jesus in the mix, too. Maybe He can make some things better.*

Then God spoke again to my heart: "A relationship with Me was never meant to be an addition; it's an *exchange*." It's about a person surrendering everything they are to receive everything He is.

Following Christ is not about making Him *one* priority among many; it is about making Him *the* priority.

Following Christ is not about making Him *one* priority among many; it is about making Him *the* priority. It is not about giving Him *part* of our lives; it is about giving Him *all* of who we are. If we truly want to experience God, we must come to Him with a willingness to make that exchange—our life for His.

So often this is where we falter. We try to engage God with the wrong mindset. We really want everything Jesus offers, but we aren't willing to relinquish complete control. The mere thought of yielding all control to Christ instantly causes our minds to fill with irrational fears. *What if He doesn't do a good job? What if He keeps me from good things? What if He fails me?* As if a loving God who has already proven His love through such great sacrifice would ever fail us. Yet we feel much safer when we hold the reins. So we try to "add Jesus in" to our lives while still maintaining control, which of course produces little or no results.

We must redefine our understanding of what it means to follow Jesus. There really is no option that allows us to maintain control of our lives and follow Jesus, too. Following Jesus doesn't work that way. Once we accept how the relationship works—we give Him complete control and He then utilizes that control to lead us to fullness of life—it makes following Jesus much simpler. You stop trying to analyze every situation to see if it makes sense first before you follow Him, and cease taking back control when the going gets tough. Once you've made up your mind that following Jesus means making Him Lord of all, you are free to simply follow, trusting that He will lead you in the right direction, even if it doesn't make sense initially.

Perhaps you have even tried giving Jesus control a time or two without really settling this concept of *the exchange* in your mind. You may start out okay, but inevitably at some point you will feel He is leading you down a path that seems too costly and you will take back control. Then we reason that our initial fears about giving Jesus control were right. If we follow Him in radical obedience, it won't be worth it. It will be too dangerous and cost us the things we love most in life.

To experience Jesus, we must relinquish our right of control in every area of life.

So we have a problem on our hands: We want the abundant life that Jesus promises us, but we don't want to give Him total control of our lives. What do we do?

More often than not, we try to carve out a comfortable place in our lives for Jesus to reign while *we* continue to rule in the really important areas.

Unfortunately, this will never work. We will never truly experience God in this way. To experience Jesus, we must relinquish our right of control in every area of life. As much as we may *want* it to work another way, it won't. Luke 16:13 clearly states, "No servant can serve two masters."

Thankfully, when we forfeit control, we are giving control to a loving, all-powerful God who will do a much better job than we ever could. If we are going to gain Him and His abundant life, we must let go.

It reminds me of watching *Tarzan* as a kid. Do you remember him—the human raised by monkeys? He lived in the jungle and got around by swinging from one vine to the next. Imagine Tarzan's journey through the jungle being similar to how God wants to guide us through life. Just as Tarzan would swing from vine to vine on the way to his destination, God wants to lead us from experience to experience on the way to our destination.

At the beginning of our faith journey, we are hanging on with both hands to a single vine. This vine could represent our life. We can't make any progress while both hands are clasped tightly to our lives, but there is a feeling of familiarity and control as we cling to our little vine.

Jesus then shows us a series of vines in front of us that represent the path He desires to guide us down. We know we want to follow Him, so we begin. We swing over a little bit and when we are close enough, we let go with one hand and grab the second vine. Jesus says, "Good! Now let go of your life completely, grab the next vine, and we'll be off on our journey together."

> **The only way to have**
> **true life is to let go.**

This is where many get stuck. We realize that to keep moving forward, we have to let go of the first vine. But we are afraid to let go because it is all we have ever known, and that familiarity provides us with a false sense of security. Even though fearfully clinging to it only keeps us from the good things God has in store for us, our fear of the uncertain keeps us holding on. We are unwilling to let go and continue on our journey, so we stay there—one hand on the first vine and one on the second, stuck in the same place.

It's not that we don't have a hold of God—we do, if we have believed the gospel. However, we're not going anywhere. We're not experiencing much, if anything, because we are unwilling to let go of what is familiar and secure. We see the next vines that God is calling us toward, and we want to move, but our fear of letting go of what we have keeps us from moving forward.

Too many of us live this way! The crazy thing is that Jesus tells us that if we keep holding on to our lives, we are going to lose them anyway (Matthew 16:25). The only way to have true life is to let go.

God is not asking us to give Him control so He can harm us. On the contrary, He asks for our surrender because He longs to use us and lead us to a full, abundant life. However, if we don't surrender to His call and let Him guide us, we will never get there. Left to ourselves, we inevitably remain clinging to the first vine, frustrated at our lack of experiencing God's goodness.

If your current commitment to Jesus is different from what He outlines in His Word, this could explain why you haven't experienced God the way you desire.

Unsurprisingly, *surrender* is one of the central themes of the New Testament. In fact, whenever Jesus called someone into relationship with Him, He asked them to follow Him and completely reorient their life around His lordship. Let's look at a few Scriptures that describe this level of surrender:

- "Then he said to them all: 'If anyone would come after me, he must deny himself and take up his cross daily and follow me.'" (Luke 9:23)

- "If you try to hang on to your life, you will lose it. But if you give up your life for my sake, you will save it." (Matthew 16:25 NLT)

- "Any of you who does not give up everything he has cannot be my disciple." (Luke 14:33)

As you can see, this is a pretty radical call Jesus has given us. His instructions couldn't be clearer: "If you trust me with your life and follow the instructions I have given you, I promise I will lead you to the abundant life you so desperately desire."

The question is: Does your commitment level resemble the commitment level that Jesus speaks of in the previous verses? If your current commitment to Jesus is different from what He outlines in His Word, this could explain why you haven't experienced God the way you desire.

God is looking for people who will leave everything and follow Him wholeheartedly. Luke 14:25–26 reports, "Large crowds were traveling with Jesus, and turning to them he said: 'If anyone comes to me and does not hate his father and mother, his wife and children, his brothers and sisters—yes, even his own life—he cannot be my disciple.'" The word *hate* in this verse doesn't mean to dislike, but to "love less." What Jesus is really saying is this: *Anyone who comes to Me and doesn't love even the best things in their life less than Me cannot be My disciple.*

The message in these verses is clear: The only way to truly experience Jesus is to follow Him, surrendering each day to whatever He asks of us.

You may be thinking, *There's no way I could ever live like that! Even if I wanted to, I would fail.* Don't worry! God knows you won't be perfect. No one is. Even when we live in complete surrender, we will still make mistakes. Surrender is not living a perfect life, it is maintaining an attitude of the heart where we continually allow God to lead, instruct, and mold our lives as He desires.

It Worked for Them

I am always motivated when I look at how much the disciples experienced God. They had joy in persecution, peace in trials, and God's power poured through their lives on a regular basis.

Because they responded to God exactly the way He asked, they experienced God exactly the way He promised.

Have you ever wondered why they seemed to experience so much of God's abundant life? I believe the answer is fairly simple. When Jesus asked them to sell out to Him, they did it! Check out the following verses:

- "So they pulled their boats up on shore, left everything and followed him." (Luke 5:11)

- "After this, Jesus went out and saw a tax collector by the name of Levi sitting at his tax booth. 'Follow me,' Jesus said to him, and Levi got up, left everything and followed him." (Luke 5:27–28)

The above verses highlight the kind of surrender the disciples responded with when Jesus called them. They were willing to instantly change whatever was necessary in order to shape their lives around Jesus—even to the point of walking away from their jobs and businesses!

God may not be calling you to leave your physical location to follow Him, but the point I want you to see here is that when Jesus called them to surrender completely to Him, they did it. This was the key! Because they responded to God exactly the way He asked, they experienced God exactly the way He promised.

As we surrender to Him just like the Bible outlines and as His disciples did, we too can experience Him to the degree they did! Romans 2:11 says, "God does not show favoritism." He will respond to us just like He did to the disciples, if we will respond to Him in the same way they did. That's why He gave us all these examples and promises in His Word—not to frustrate us or discourage us, but to prove to us that it really works! If we make it a priority each day to give Him our lives, we will experience Him and His promises just like He said we would.

Explosion!

It's kind of like a chemical reaction. In case you accidentally fell asleep in science class, this is where you mix different chemicals together and study the responses. If you have ever had the chance to try this, you know that if you take one element or compound and then take turns mixing it with other elements and compounds, you will get completely different reactions. For example, if you mix fire with water, what happens? The fire will go out. But if you take that same fire and mix it with gasoline, what happens? You get an explosion. Those are two *completely* different responses. The fire was the same in both scenarios, but what it was mixed with caused a completely different reaction.

If we mix Jesus' call to surrender with the action of wholehearted surrender, it's like mixing fire and gasoline—and our experience with God explodes.

It's the same with God. His call to total surrender is like that fire. Depending on how we respond to His call, our level of experience with Him will completely change. When we take God's *call* for wholehearted surrender and then mix it with the *action* of half-hearted surrender, it's like mixing fire with water. Not much happens, except the fire being extinguished.

But if we mix Jesus' call to surrender with the action of wholehearted surrender, it's like mixing fire and gasoline—and our experience with God explodes.

Jesus' call to complete surrender has not changed. The same invitation that went out to the disciples two thousand years ago is the same call that goes out to each of us today. Jesus says, "You give Me the entirety of your life that is doomed to sin, death, and eternity in hell. In return, I will forgive your sins, heal your heart, lead you in the path of true life, and you will spend all of eternity with Me in heaven." Just like every human on the face of the earth, we must determine for ourselves how we will respond to that call.

Solving Your Rubik's Cube

Our response to God's call for complete surrender will be the single greatest determining factor in how we experience Him. It may seem funny but this whole process reminds me of a toy I used to have when I was young called . . . the Rubik's Cube. You know, the little square thing with six sides, each side with nine different colors on it. The whole point is to take the cube with all the colors mixed up and then twist the rows of the cube left, right, and up and down until all the colors are back on the same side . . . and this was supposed to be fun. If you're like me, you twisted that cube in every direction for a couple of hours—before throwing it down in frustration. It seemed impossible to figure out which way to twist that cube to make those colors line up again!

Our response to God's call for complete surrender will be the single greatest determining factor in how we experience Him.

Trying to figure out our lives can be like trying to figure out that Rubik's cube—frustrating. Since all of us were born into sin (Romans 5:12), it's like we inherited a messed-up Rubik's Cube in the form of our lives, and we're trying to solve it. As most of us have noticed, this can be pretty hard! Just as we would twist and turn the cube trying to figure it out, we twist and turn our lives. We make certain decisions and try all kinds of things hoping they will bring us more happiness or a better life. We hope that all these decisions we make each day will bring our lives closer to "lining up" the way they should. However, far too often our effort doesn't seem to get us any closer to solving things—and often we mess things up even more.

As impossible as it seems to figure out a Rubik's Cube (I have never been able to do it), figuring out our lives is infinitely harder. In fact, on our own it is impossible. Fortunately, God has a plan for each person's life (Jeremiah 29:11). He has a vision for every color in our lives to align in perfect harmony with His design. Since God is the only one who knows the plan for our lives, no matter how hard we try to figure it out on our own, we will fail (Proverbs 20:24).

God knows exactly how to put our lives back together. No matter how messed up our lives are, He can tell us at each step exactly which way to turn. God is waiting for us to submit to His leadership and allow Him to guide us through life.

The Other Side of the Coin

I hope it's becoming clear to you that surrender is the only path to experiencing the good things God has in store. However, there is another side to the coin. While it is true that abundant life will be ours if we surrender all to Christ, it is also true that if we choose to keep areas of our lives away from His control, by default we submit those areas to the Enemy. That may not be our intention, but the truth is that every action of our lives serves either God or Satan. There is no middle ground. When we submit to God, we come under

His protection, but when we submit to the Enemy, we give him permission to work in our lives. John 10:10 reveals to us what the Enemy desires to do in every situation: "steal, kill and destroy."

So when we choose not to surrender to Christ, we do more than just miss out on the good things God desires for us. We also make ourselves vulnerable to the Enemy's destructive plans. Unfortunately, as we'll see in the next chapter, this is something I know all too well.

Questions

1. What have you learned about the type of commitment Jesus is looking for from those who follow Him?

2. If you had to choose only one of the two words to describe your commitment to Christ, would *addition* or *exchange* be more accurate?

3. Can you identify areas in your life that you have yet to submit to God's control?

4. What is holding you back from submitting those areas to Christ's control?

chapter 4

my story

The principles we've been talking about aren't abstract truths in the Bible—they are truths we *experience* in our lives. Let me share a little of my story with you.

Like many families today, my father and mother divorced when I was very young. When I was about a year old, my mother remarried. My stepfather was a great man of God who gave our family a Christian foundation. We went to church every Sunday as a family, and I knew all the exciting Bible stories like Jonah and the big fish and David and Goliath. My parents loved each other and everything in our family seemed perfect.

My siblings and I slept
on foam mats on the floor.

About midway through grade school, our family hit some very tough times financially. We couldn't afford our own place anymore, so we moved in with my grandparents. I have great memories of living there, but we lived on very little. My siblings and I slept on foam mats on the floor of my grandparents' dining room and all of my worldly possessions fit in two little cubbies in their laundry room.

My grandparents lived in a rich neighborhood, so all the kids I went to school with were very well-off. They came to school wearing the latest designer clothes and playing with the coolest new electronic gadgets. As you might guess, that wasn't the case for me. As a result I became an outcast. From fourth through sixth grade, people at that school picked on me mercilessly. Every recess was torture. No matter how hard I tried, I never seemed to be able to gain their approval or escape their cruelty.

By the end of my sixth-grade year, insecurity was eating away at the inside of my heart like a well-developed cancer.

Shifting Who's on the Throne

By the time I reached middle school, our family was doing a little better financially and we were able to move out of my grandparents' house to a home of our own—and a new school! I remember being so excited at the chance to start over. More than anything, I wanted to make friends and be accepted.

One thought raced around and around my head: "No matter what, people are going to like me now."

When I had to choose between Jesus and the acceptance of others, I chose acceptance.

At the time, I had no idea just how life-changing that determination would prove to be. I had made the subtle decision that gaining the approval of others would now be the top priority in my life. Up until that time, I had always placed Jesus in that position. I didn't purposely choose to dethrone Jesus, but by choosing to pursue acceptance above all, that's exactly what I did. I still tried to follow Jesus, too—it's just that when I had to choose between Jesus and the acceptance of others, I chose acceptance.

By the time I was in eighth grade, this shift on the throne of my life was already causing terrible results. I was constantly in trouble in school. I wasn't breaking the law or anything, but I became the class clown. I was loud and disruptive and spent pretty much every day after school in detention. I really didn't mind the trouble I got in, though, because whenever people laughed at my antics, I took that as a form of acceptance. Things got so bad that two months into my eighth-grade year, I had been given more detentions than there were days of school! Finally, I made one of my teachers so mad she told the principal I was the most disruptive student she had taught in twenty-five years. The principal decided to expel me from school and I was forced to finish eighth grade at a private school.

As I entered high school, the price of popularity kept moving me further and further away from the path of following Jesus. In my ninth-grade year, I began partying and getting high. By the time I was a sophomore I was getting high pretty much every day. From that time on I rarely, if ever, missed a day of getting high until the day I graduated.

It is important to note that throughout this time I still prayed. I still considered myself a Christian. On occasion I even told my friends that every person needed a relationship with Jesus!

It's not that I didn't believe in God, or even that He had no influence in my life. I simply wasn't allowing Him to be *Lord*, to rule on the throne of my life. As a result, I didn't experience God much in those days. There were times when I felt God speak to me or felt His guidance in my life, but without a doubt I missed many experiences with Him during those years. There were so many hardships I endured needlessly because of my failure to trust God. My disobedience caused me to miss many opportunities that God had in store for me. These experiences continue to serve as a reminder to me of what happens when we choose to camp way down the slope of the mountain.

However, as far as my plan for acceptance was concerned, things worked like a charm. I became an extremely popular kid in high school. I dated the prettiest girls, was successful in sports, and despite my drug usage I even managed to get good grades. People told me in high school, "Mike, you are the reason why marijuana should be legalized. Look at you—you get high every day, but you still get great grades in school, and you start both ways on the football team. Man, your life is a success!"

What they didn't see was the gaping hole of insecurity that ran right through the middle of my life. Nothing seemed to fill it. You see, I chose to deal with my insecurities on my own instead of letting Christ lead me. I thought I knew what was best for me. Since I had been hurt by the constant jeering I endured in grade school, I was sure that what I *really* needed to feel whole again was acceptance.

God said, "Mike, what are you doing with your life?"

But as I mentioned earlier, when we don't follow Christ, by default we are following the Enemy, and that will always lead to destruction in our lives. I was no exception. As I fed my desire for acceptance, the desire grew stronger and stronger until it became a monster that controlled me. Even when I "succeeded" and became popular, the wound in my heart remained open. No matter how many people told me I was cool, or how many girls paid attention to me, it never satisfied for long. I woke up the next day feeling just as insecure as the day before. The emptiness *always* returned.

Looking back, it is easy to see that I was completely controlled by my craving for approval and acceptance. In short, I was a slave to sin.

The Encounter

It was spring break of my senior year when God began to deal with me. On the outside, everything seemed great. I had a beautiful girlfriend, I was popular, my grades were good; all seemed well. One night over the break, I got high on a couple of different things and was about to pass out for the night on my friend's floor. Even in that horrible state, God spoke to me. Out of nowhere I felt Him speak clearly in my mind. God said, "Mike, what are you doing with your life?" Those words pierced me to my core. Deep inside, I knew what I was doing was wrong, but I wasn't willing to part with my sin. I was convinced that giving up my sin and following Jesus would make me more miserable than I already was.

As God's words pierced my heart, I began to think back on my childhood. From a young age I always felt like I would do something great for the Lord. Even during my years of getting high, I continued to picture myself turning things around and serving God. However, as I lay on the floor, I had to face the facts: I was about to graduate, and I had no job, no money, no driver's license, and no idea of where I was going to college. I remember thinking, *Everyone in high school thinks I'm cool, but once I graduate people will see what a loser I really am.*

I knew in that moment that my life needed to change. Over the next few months, I tried to change with my own strength. I wasn't willing to let God lead my life yet, so I maintained control while trying to live a little more like I thought Jesus would want me to.

As you can imagine, this wasn't super successful. The summer after I graduated from high school, I managed to quit getting high for two straight weeks. This was a *major* accomplishment for me. So I figured I would reward myself by getting high—what a brilliant idea! A friend and I got high and went to a movie. I still remember the events that followed so clearly. Shortly after the movie began, I started to experience some irregularities with my heart. It would take several beats normally and then it would stop for a few seconds, and then it would beat normally again and then stop. I started to feel light-headed, and within a minute or two, the left side of my body became numb. Nervously, I turned to my friend and told him that I couldn't feel my face. He thought that sounded hilarious and started laughing at me. After another minute or two, I was really panicking. I wondered if I was having a stroke and would be paralyzed on my left side.

"God, I don't care what You have to do to me. I need to change."

Instantly, my future flashed before my eyes. I thought of how I wanted to go to college and play sports—what if I could never walk again? I considered what all my years of living for myself had gotten me. The foolishness of my choices was suddenly evident as I took inventory of my life. I realized that if *I* kept controlling my life, I would end up destroying myself.

Right there in the middle of that movie theater I finally gave God what He has asked of every human since Adam and Eve: complete lordship of every area of my life.

I told the Lord, "God, I don't care what You have to do to

me. I need to change. Whatever it takes God, do it. Even if You have to take me to jail, fine. Nothing is off limits anymore. I'm Yours."

About the time I finished that prayer, the sensations I was feeling in my body slowly lifted, and then I passed out. At the end of the movie I woke up feeling perfectly fine. As I walked out, I tried to make sense of everything that had just happened. Right away the Enemy whispered in my head, "Come on, Mike, don't be weird, it was just a little allergic reaction or something. Don't do anything rash. It's no big deal."

But then I felt the Lord speak to me and say, "Mike, what is it going to take before you listen to Me?" In that moment I was completely honest with the Lord. I knew He already knew my heart, so I told Him, "God, I know I need to change and somewhere deep down I know I want to. But honestly, on the surface I don't want to change. I *want* to want to change, though. I really want to have the desire to live the way You want me to, but I just don't know that I am there right now."

As it turns out, that was the last day I ever got high.

I continued to pray, asking, "God, will You change what I want and make it line up with what You want?" After confessing my state to Him and asking for His help, I reaffirmed the commitment I made to Him before I passed out and told Him again, "God, whatever You have to do to make me who You want me to be, do it. Nothing is off limits anymore."

The Difference
True Surrender Makes

When I said all this to God, I didn't feel any fireworks or hear heavenly music. There were no otherworldly sensations. To be honest, I was skeptical about whether anything would change or if I would just take back control of my life at the first opportunity. However, something happens the moment we finally respond sincerely to God's call for the complete surrender of our lives.

As it turns out, that was the last day I ever got high. Most sins in my life I have had to struggle to overcome, but that was one that God simply took from me. I immediately started reading my Bible and praying. No one was forcing me to; I just decided if I was going to do this Jesus thing, I was going to do it with all my heart.

Over time, I had to change all my friends. I tried to keep hanging out with my old friends for a while, but all they did every night was party and get high. If you've ever been the only sober person around a bunch of high people, you know it gets old really fast. So I finally told them that I loved them, but I had to go a new direction in my life. I wasn't mean to them. I didn't tell them they were going to hell or anything. I simply explained what God had done in my heart and that I needed to change my life.

I began to cry out to God for Christian friends. There was a tough period between leaving my old friends and finding new ones in which I felt lonely and isolated. But eventually, God brought me to a church where I met some great friends who helped me grow. Little by little, God began to root out my old habits. He dealt with my life one area at a time, careful not to overwhelm me.

I had been going to church twice a week for six months, reading my Bible and praying every day, before God convicted me of my cussing habit. One day I simply realized, "If I'm a Christian, I probably shouldn't be cussing every other word." Cussing was wrong the whole time, but God was working on other issues like my drug habit first. When I was ready, He moved on to something else, and He continues that process in my life to this day. I still laugh when I think about what my new Christian friends must have thought: *Who is this guy? He's seeking God with all his heart, devouring his Bible, and going to church every time the doors open—and then shares about the work God is doing in his life with cuss words for emphasis?*

In the nearly two decades since that summer evening in the movie theater, I have watched God transform my life from a drug-using, insecure loser into someone He uses to share His grace and love with people all across the globe. This complete transformation didn't happen because I was special, but because I was finally willing to let God lead me. Though it looks different for each of us, God will bring this magnitude of transformation into any life willing to fully surrender to Him. God is a God of hope and possibility who can't wait for His children to trust in His leadership.

What About You?

If you choose to embark on the same journey of daily surrender to the lordship of Jesus, it won't be long before you have your own story of transformation. You, too, will experience example after example of God's promises and presence becoming real in your life. That's just who God is. He always desires to lead us to fullness of life.

He strongly desires to be good to you and lead you to fullness of life.

Looking back, I see that my biggest error was not trusting that God really wanted to give me a life full of love, satisfaction, freedom, joy, and peace. So in my fear, I took my life into my own hands—but that was really placing my life in the hands of the Enemy who tried his best to destroy me.

Perhaps you are wrestling with the idea of complete surrender and you feel the same fear I did. Realize that God is not asking you to give Him control so that He can harm you. On the contrary, He asks for your surrender because He strongly desires to be good to you and lead you to fullness of life. Jeremiah 29:11 says, "'For I know the plans I have for you,' declares the Lord, 'plans to prosper you and not to harm you, plans to give you hope and a future.'"

Complete surrender is the only path that will lead you to the fulfillment of God's good plans in your life. There may come times when the directions God gives you seem very difficult. You may even be tempted to question His leadership, convincing yourself that this time His directions will surely steal from your life instead of add to it. In those moments, you have to trust that God really *does* have your best interest at heart, even if you can't see the big picture yet.

I think we tend to see the surrender of our lives as something that benefits God at our expense. This erroneous viewpoint will only cause us to resist or mistrust the process. God is not asking us to surrender for His benefit. He's really not. After all, there is nothing we can add to God. It is for *our* benefit that He asks us to surrender! He really is a loving Father who simply wants the best for us, His children. He knows that the best results our lives could ever have will come when He is leading. This is why He asks us to surrender. He wants the absolute best for us in this life and the next.

Every instruction God gives you is like a treasure map that leads to a fuller, more abundant life. The bottom line is, *When you follow God's instructions you will experience Him more; when you ignore God's instructions you will experience Him less.* It's as simple as that. You may not understand each turn along the way, but your destination will be more amazing than you ever dared to imagine.

Questions

1. The seeds of my struggle with insecurity were planted when I was very young. Looking back at your life, how has the Enemy tried to plant destructive patterns in your life? What effect has it had on you?

2. I had to walk away from my old lifestyle and friends. What would you have to walk away from in your life if you were to surrender all to God?

3. Even though walking away from some things in your life may be hard, can you really say that you believe God will transform your life for the better? Or, if you are honest, do you fear what He may do with your life if you give it all to Him?

4. What steps could you take to build the kind of trust necessary to surrender the areas you hold back most from the Lord?

chapter 5

God's treasure map

My friends Matt and Crystal were very much in love. They had been dating for a while and decided they were ready to commit to each other for life. Behind the scenes, Matt began thinking of creative ways to propose. Hoping to make it a wonderful experience for her, he worked hard and devised an elaborate plan.

When the time came to set his plan in motion, Matt summoned Crystal to a certain place and when she arrived, there waiting for her was a clue. This clue turned out to be part of a series of clues he had set up for her to follow. Like a step-by-step treasure map, each clue led her to a place that had been significant in their relationship.

It didn't take Crystal long to guess what treasure was waiting for her at the end of that treasure map! Finally she came to the last stop. There stood Matt, anxiously awaiting her arrival. He dropped to one knee, asked Crystal to be his wife, and sealed the commitment by placing a beautiful ring on her finger.

Like any treasure map, God's map must be followed before His treasure is experienced.

Isn't that story like our walk with God? God loves us so much that He has given us clues in His Word so we can discover the great things He has in store for us. Like Matt at the end of his treasure map, God eagerly waits for us to follow His instructions so He can share His overwhelming treasures with us. Our job is simply to follow the map.

A Treasure Map for Every Treasure

Too often we fall into the trap of viewing the Bible as a boring, restrictive book that is there to limit our fun and prevent us from living an exciting life. This is a lie straight from the Enemy. The Bible really is a treasure map given to us by God so we can experience a full and abundant life. Every instruction is like a priceless direction on the map that will reward us richly if we follow it. Once we realize this, it will completely change our perspective on the Bible. Reading the Bible will excite us when we realize that its instructions lead us to a better life.

But like any treasure map, God's map must be followed before His treasure is experienced. Too often we sit around wondering why we don't experience more of God's treasures —yet we have never taken the time to follow His map. All God's promises are true, but they cannot be experienced when we stay where we are and ignore His command to follow. For example, consider the following Scripture:

- "Delight yourself in the Lord and he will give you the desires of your heart." (Psalm 37:4)

Can you see the treasure map in this verse? God is showing us how to have the desires of our hearts—what a priceless treasure! Think about the billions of dollars and hours that are spent by people every day trying to fulfill the desires of their hearts, yet they still fall short. God tells us that the path to this treasure is to delight ourselves in the Lord. Can you see how it works now? God gives us a promise—that we will be given the desires of our heart. Then He tells us how to get it—by delighting ourselves in Him. If we are willing to follow the map, we will have the treasure!

To delight yourself in the Lord means that you treasure Him, pursue Him, spend time with Him, make Him a priority.

Perhaps you are thinking, *Mike, this simply can't be true because I'm a Christian, and God is not giving me the desires of my heart right now!* My first question to you would be, "Can you honestly say that you are *delighting* yourself in the Lord?" That's the treasure map you must follow first if you are going to experience this particular treasure.

It's important to understand, this verse is not an open promise that every Christian will always be given the desires of their heart. It is a promise only to those who *choose* to delight themselves in the Lord. We must understand that if we are not delighting ourselves in the Lord, this promise does not apply to us. We often read a promise in the Bible and automatically assume it should apply to us—even if we aren't following the map's instructions. But it simply doesn't work that way. Treasure isn't found by those who receive a map and do not follow it. Treasure is only found by those willing to follow the map to its destination. This false expectation that God's promises should be ours even when we don't follow His Word is responsible for much of why our experience with God falls short of what is available to us.

I can personally testify to the truth of this psalm. To delight yourself in the Lord means that you treasure Him, pursue Him, spend time with Him, make Him a priority, and value His direction in your life. I have found that if I delight myself in the Lord in these ways, He provides the desires of my heart.

The process usually looks something like this: I notice myself in a state of anxiousness caused by unmet expectations or desires. When I realize what is going on, I always try to get alone with the Lord and pour out my heart to Him. When I first come to Him, my heart is full of all kinds of com-

peting desires. Some are good, some are not. But as I arrange
my life so that I delight myself in the Lord, God begins to help
me navigate the desires in my heart. He exposes any fleshly,
selfish desires lurking in me and reveals them for what they
are: dead-end roads that will only leave my heart empty, even
if I were to achieve them.

With my false desires pushed aside, God is then able to
steer my focus to the desires of my heart that truly need to be
fulfilled. As He continues to guide my heart, I find that *my
deepest desires become the very things God desires for me.*
As I delight myself in Him, our desires become one. Once my
heart is in that state, it becomes His pleasure to grant every
one of my desires. I have watched God guide me through this
process countless times.

Let me give you a couple more examples of this concept
from Scripture:

- "But seek first his kingdom and his righteousness, and all
these things will be given to you as well." (Matthew 6:33)

Can you see the treasure map more easily this time? The
treasure is "all these things will be given to you as well." What
does "all these things" refer to? In the verses before this one,
Jesus is teaching about how often we run around half-crazy
trying to provide for ourselves, whether it is food or clothes
or possessions that we feel we need. Oftentimes, our pursuit
of "these things" becomes so strong that we sacrifice putting
God's kingdom first in our lives.

Jesus is saying, "If you seek Me first, you don't need to
worry about those other things—I'll make sure you have them."

What an amazing treasure! God promises that if we seek Him first, He will always make a way for us to have the resources we need to live.

Without God's direction we dive into all kinds of things that only end up hurting us.

However, just like we saw in Psalm 37:4, this is not a blanket promise of God's provision to everyone. It is a promise with a requirement: to seek first His kingdom. Learning to seek first His kingdom is the treasure map we must follow if we are to receive this treasure.

- "The Lord will withhold no good thing from those who do what is right." (Psalm 84:11 NLT)

I trust you already have this one figured out. The treasure is that God will withhold no good thing from us. The treasure map is doing what is right, or learning to walk consistently in the truth God reveals to us. I would rather have this treasure than all the money in the world!

So often we don't know what's good for us. We *think* we do, but without God's direction we dive into all kinds of things that only end up hurting us. Knowing God has promised to provide every good thing we need keeps us looking to Him instead of searching for what we think might be good on our own.

For example, on our honeymoon my wife and I booked a weeklong stay at a resort in Jamaica. I saved my money and reserved us a little bungalow right on the beach. I was so excited I would look at pictures of our bungalow online several times a week leading up to the honeymoon—I couldn't wait to actually be there with Alicia!

The day of our wedding finally arrived, and the next morning we set off for Jamaica. After a long day of traveling, we arrived at the resort—only to be told that our bungalow was not available. The hotel had made a mistake and we would not be able to access the room until the next day. Furthermore, the only other room available that night was a little room right next to the road with an air conditioner that sounded like a lawnmower. And worst of all . . . it had two single beds! Not exactly what I envisioned for my honeymoon.

The resort was very apologetic and gave us a $200 credit toward an excursion of our choice. The next day we went to the excursion table and signed up to go deep-sea fishing. Two days later the time came for our fishing trip. We got on the boat full of excitement at the thought of wrestling in a big one out on the open seas. As we set out from shore I remember thinking, *What could be better? We're in Jamaica on our honeymoon, deep-sea fishing, the weather is great—this will be the perfect day.*

Within about five minutes of that thought, both Alicia and I became extremely sick. After sharing with the ocean everything we had for breakfast, we begged them to take us back to shore. But because there were other passengers, we were stuck—for *three hours.*

After what seemed like an eternity, we finally made it

back to shore. We collapsed onto our beds and slept for several hours. After we recovered, we agreed: Had we known in advance how awful our experience would be, we would have paid $200 *not* to go!

We must realize that in life our foresight is severely limited. Alicia and I thought for sure that fishing was going to be a great experience for us, but the opposite was true. Think about how many times this has been the case in your life. Have you ever been sure something was going to be great, only to see it turn out badly in the end? On the other hand, think about all the things you were certain would not be good for you that ended up being great experiences.

Would we expect to experience a mountaintop view if we weren't willing to climb the mountain?

The point is this: God promises that if we are diligent to walk in His ways and do what is right, He will provide every good thing we need and help us steer clear of life's potential pitfalls. What an invaluable treasure! After all, God's the only one who sees and knows everything, so what better Guide could we hope for? We simply have to be willing to follow His map.

Something for Nothing

If we are not experiencing God, it is an important milestone when we come to realize that He is not the one to blame. His promises are all true and can be experienced by anyone who chooses to follow His instructions. If we have not been experiencing God, the most likely reason is that we have been unwilling to surrender and follow His treasure map.

It's almost as if we come to Christ and say, "I want to experience all of your promises—every single one! Oh, and thank You so much for giving me a treasure map that teaches me how to get there, Jesus. There's just one thing—can I have the treasure without following the map?"

What would happen if we applied this same logic to any other area of life? Would we expect to experience a mountaintop view if we weren't willing to climb the mountain? Are we going to experience the rush of a live concert if we aren't willing to purchase a ticket? Would we expect to enjoy the warmth of a hot shower if we're not willing to turn on the water? Like every other area of life, our experience of God requires certain things of us.

Jesus makes available to us blessings that we cannot acquire on our own, blessings like peace, forgiveness, salvation, and joy. Then He comes to us and tells us through His Word, "I love you and I want you to find the true life I have purchased for you! I want you to have all of it. Let me show you how to receive it. You simply have to follow me, *wherever* I lead. I know it will be hard at times, so I am sending My Spirit to be with you and help you do it!"

Instead of rejoicing at this amazing offer—and then doing what is necessary to receive it—too often we demand the blessings without doing what Jesus tells us. Then, because we choose not to follow Jesus, we don't experience the blessings He promises us—and we actually blame Him!

The close of this chapter is an important landmark on our journey through this book. Until now, I have tried to help you identify whether, like most Christians, you are missing out on much of the abundant life Jesus has made available to you—and whether that lack is because you aren't willing to surrender to Jesus and follow His treasure map.

But we must go deeper. I have found that even when we have internalized this information and want to make a change, something still seems to hinder us from surrendering and consistently choosing the path He has laid out for us.

Most often where we falter is not in our revelation, but in our application. We know what we need to do. It's when we actually try to do it that we stumble.

Perhaps you've seen this in your own life. God convicts you in an area and then shows you how you need to live. You know He is right, and you are anxious to obey Him and get your life back on track. Then when the opportunity comes to actually do it, you fail. Again, and again . . . and again. Perhaps, like so many, you have spent more than a few moments feeling like a failure and wondering, *Why is this surrender thing so hard?!* If we believe that Jesus is real, and if, to the best of our knowledge, we believe that trusting Him with our lives will turn out for the best, then why can't we *do it*?

The answer is in our next chapter. I believe what I have come to call "the original deception" is the number one thing that derails us as we try to live out a life of submission to Christ. Overcoming this deception of the Enemy is the key to surrender and finally experiencing God the way we have all been seeking.

Questions

1. What, honestly, has been your view of the Bible in the past?

2. Does it change your motivation to read and apply God's Word knowing that through His Word He is giving you instructions that lead to perfect treasures?

3. Have you ever followed an instruction in God's Word and saw it lead to treasure in your life? If so, what happened?

4. Have you ever ignored an instruction in God's Word and found yourself in trouble?

5. What instructions from God's Word can you begin applying right now to start seeing more of God's promises fulfilled in your life?

chapter 6

the original deception

The original deception was the very first trick the Enemy used on Eve in the garden of Eden to cause her to fall into sin—and it is the same trick he uses on us today. If we can dispel this original deception, we will be able to walk in the type of surrender Jesus asks for and begin to experience Him in amazing ways.

To see how this original deception works, we have to go way back to the beginning of the Bible. In the book of Genesis, we find the Devil's first encounter with the human race:

- Now the serpent was more crafty than any of the wild animals the Lord God had made. He said to the woman, "Did God really say, 'You must not eat from any tree in the garden'?" The woman said to the serpent, "We may eat fruit from the trees in the garden, but God did say, 'You must not eat fruit from the tree that is in the middle of the garden, and you must not touch it, or you will die.'" "You will not surely die," the serpent said to the woman. "For God knows that when you eat of it your eyes will be opened, and you will be like God, knowing good and evil." When the woman saw that the fruit of the tree was good for food and pleasing to the eye, and also desirable for gaining wisdom, she took some and ate it. She also gave some to her husband, who was with her, and he ate it. (Genesis 3:1–6)

Let's break this down. God has created a garden for humans to live in. They have everything they could ever need or want. Adam and Eve are able to walk with God and talk with Him face-to-face. There is an abundance of food and beauty. They don't have to work hard for money to survive. They don't have to worry about tan lines. They can simply enjoy God and the world He created for them.

Satan is always looking for an opportunity to offer up suggestions aimed at tainting the way we see God.

In order to preserve the blessed life He has provided them, God gives them some specific instructions. There is a certain tree in the middle of the garden from which God tells them not to eat. God knows that horrible consequences will come from eating from this tree and disobeying His instructions, so in His love He warns them not to do it.

Then Satan enters the scene, and with one conversation Eve is willing to abandon this great life God has given her and dive into sin. Why? What happened? How did Satan convince her to throw away the life God had given her? Enter *the original deception.*

In verse 1, Satan comes up to Eve and says something like, "Wow, Eve, look at all the great fruit trees in this garden. This is amazing! I can't believe God would say you shouldn't eat from any of these trees in the garden. They sure look good to me."

Notice how Satan begins. He doesn't try to tempt her to eat the forbidden fruit right away. He knows that as long as her trust in God and His loving intentions for her are firmly intact she'll never give way to sin. So He subtly goes to work, hoping to destroy her trust. He offers up a suggestion that is meant to paint God as a restrictive tyrant instead of a trustworthy, loving God. He says, "Did God really say, 'You must not eat from any tree in the garden'?" This, of course, is not at all what God said. God didn't say she couldn't eat of *any* tree; He just warned her about the *one* tree in the middle of the garden. One of the tools Satan uses to try to open our hearts to the original deception is lies or half-truths intended to make God's commands seem less than life-giving. Satan is always looking for an opportunity to offer up suggestions aimed at tainting the way we see God.

Perhaps you've noticed this in your life. Satan whispers in your mind, "I can't believe God would say you shouldn't have sex! Why would He want to keep you from so much joy?" The truth is, God never told us we shouldn't have sex. He simply tells us to wait until we are married. He knows that within the marriage covenant we will be free to enjoy sex without guilt or the physical and emotional dangers that accompany sex outside of marriage. You can probably think of other examples, but the danger is the same. If we don't dispel Satan's suggestion quickly with the truth, it will plant a seed of frustration toward God that will cause us to see Him as restrictive instead of loving. Satan bombards us relentlessly with these suggestions, hoping that enough will take hold in our minds to sway us away from God and toward the original deception.

To Eve's credit, she doesn't fall for it right away. In verses 2 and 3, she corrects the Devil and tells him, "God didn't say we can't eat from any of the trees in the garden. He just said we can't eat of the tree in the middle of the garden because if we do, we are going to die." (That sounds like a good reason to me!) God had obviously been very clear with Eve about why He didn't want her to eat the fruit. It wasn't that He was being overly restrictive or trying to keep her from experiencing pleasure. On the contrary, He knew that even though that fruit looked really good, it would lead to death. As I mentioned earlier, we rarely grasp how sin will affect us down the road, especially months or years later.

The same principle holds true today. God has given us His Word to tell us how to live. Why? To take our fun away? No! He wants to protect us from the terrible consequences of sin so that we can enjoy the life full of abundant blessings He has promised us.

In verses 4 and 5, Satan stops beating around the bush and

cuts right to the chase in his attempt to get Eve to doubt God's loving intentions. He basically says, "God is not trying to protect you—He is holding out on you! God knows that when you eat this fruit, you're not going to die. You will actually become wiser and more God-like. Apparently, God doesn't want that to happen, and that's why He told you not to eat the fruit. His commands are not making your life better. They are actually robbing you of the more fulfilling life you deserve!"

Once again I think if you analyze your own life, you'll see that he's trying the same approach on you. He tries to get you to bypass the faith that will trust God without question and instead reason with your natural logic to convince you that sin really is the better deal.

Satan will always try to twist the truth. His goal is to deceive you into seeing sin as something that will make your life better instead of the tool of destruction that it is.

"Sure, God encourages you to walk in purity, but how far is too far anyway? Besides, you care about him. Doesn't that make it okay? And if you don't give him what he wants, he may break up with you, and think how horrible that would be."

"Did God *really* say you shouldn't lie *ever*? I mean, just think about the consequences you'll have to face if you don't lie. Telling the truth is just not worth it this time."

"So your parents told you not to go. Big deal. They just don't understand how important this is. You know you'll have the time of your life if you go, and *everyone* is going to be there! You don't want to miss out, do you?"

Sound familiar? Satan will always try to twist the truth. His goal is to deceive you into seeing sin as something that will make your life better instead of the tool of destruction that it is. But again, more than being enticed by any one sin, it's what this thinking does to our view of God that is most dangerous long term. When we buy into Satan's lie that even some of God's instructions will end up stealing from our lives, we are making crippling assumptions about God's character.

The original deception destroys the one thing that makes surrender possible—the trust that comes from a correct view of God's character.

Since God is an all-knowing God, when we entertain the belief that some of His instructions will steal our fun or simply not be worth the price, what we are really saying is that God is *intentionally* instructing us to do things that are not in our best interest. I'm sure you can imagine how this kind of thinking affects our future decisions and how we respond to God's leading. We may not even be consciously aware of it, but when we find ourselves questioning God's instructions, Satan has already succeeded in poisoning our minds with the crux of the original deception—God simply can't be trusted. Without trust, we will form a pattern of consistently taking decisions into our own hands instead of living with the complete trust that surrender requires.

The original deception is so dangerous because by undermining our trust, it destroys the one thing necessary to experience God—surrender. Satan knows how deeply we will be transformed if we surrender all to Christ. So his main goal, if he can't keep us from knowing God altogether, is to keep us from getting to a place of complete surrender. The original deception destroys the one thing that makes surrender possible —the trust that comes from a correct view of God's character. If we view God as a loving Father whose every instruction is designed to lead us to a better life, then even when it is hard, we will obey. But if the enemy can convince us that God is a cosmic killjoy whose commands simply lead to a restrictive, boring life, we are finished. After all, why would you follow the advice of someone who meant you harm? As long as we have the wrong view of God, we will be powerless to consistently resist sin. Not necessarily because of a lack of effort, but because we lack the necessary trust in God.

Is it any wonder why we find it such a struggle to walk in daily surrender? We are trying to convince ourselves to surrender complete control of our lives to someone whose intentions we don't trust. As long as the original deception is pre: life, you will always falter in your attempts to surren you will never be able to surrender to someone you

Trust Is Key

When we trust God, we can walk in faith. Even if sin looks good to us, we will trust that God knows and wants what's best for us. We also know that our hearts are easily deceived into wanting things that are not good for us (Jeremiah 17:9). So despite the fact that sin may look good in the moment, our trust in God's good intentions creates the faith necessary to resist sin. That's why 2 Corinthians 5:7 says, "We live by faith, not by sight."

However, in the absence of trust in God, our faith is weakened. So we try to use our own logic (or "sight") to figure out what to do. This will always lead to our destruction, which is exactly why the Bible specifically instructs us not to do it. As Proverbs 3:5–6 reminds us, we should not lean on our own understanding, but in *all* our ways trust in God to direct our path.

If we go back to the story of Eve, we can see this process play out. As long as Eve is standing in faith through her trust in God, she is fine. When Satan tries to get her to eat the fruit the first time, she is not even remotely interested. She instantly shuts him down by saying, "God said we shouldn't do it." But pay close attention to what happens next.

We all know Satan persisted and tempted her a second time, and that was when she fell. But why? What changed in those few seconds between the first and second temptation? Surely the fruit didn't look any different or more tempting than the first time. Nothing had changed. So why did she suddenly give in? The only difference between the first and second time Satan tempted Eve was the way she viewed God. This one thing made all the difference, and it still does today.

The first time she viewed the situation through the eyes of trust—God is good and His every instruction was created for my benefit and protection. The second time she viewed the same situation through the eyes of the original deception—maybe God really is trying to keep me from something good, maybe He can't be trusted after all. As soon as her trust in God's character was shaken, her faith in His instructions began to falter. With her faith in God shaken, she started to rely on her own logic to figure out what to do. Since the fruit was "pleasing to the eye," Eve's own understanding suggested that the fruit was too good to pass up—and she took a bite. We all know how well that worked out for Eve—not so good. We are all still paying the consequences of that decision!

That is how sin entered the world the first time, and it is still how it enters our lives today. Our enemy continues to use the original deception to undermine our trust in God's good intentions for us. How you view God will be the greatest determining factor in whether you are able to walk in surrender or whether you will choose to rely on your own understanding.

Our View of God Affects Every Test

Let's look at a real-life example. You are in school, and it's the morning of the big test. You *meant* to study, but it just never worked out. Now here you are in first period. You're only half awake because you stayed up late playing video games with your friends. The regret starts to kick in as you sit there staring at a test that may as well be written in another language. Just as you are about to start in on your "eeny, meeny, miny, moe" approach to the multiple choice, you notice that one of the smartest people in class is sitting next to you. And his test is in plain view.

You know cheating is wrong, so you ignore the first impulse. But just like Eve, the Enemy keeps after you. "Why is it such a big deal to cheat? It's not like you cheat all the time or anything. Besides, if you fail this test, your grades will probably never recover, and if you fail the class, you will have to attend summer school to make it up. In the long run, those consequences would be much worse than anything you could face from cheating. Besides, you don't need to copy the whole test, just enough to pass. What other choice do you have?"

If you are convinced that God has given you every commandment out of His great love for you, and that they will always lead to life, then regardless of how logical it may look to sin, you will trust that following His instructions will always be best for you. You will dismiss the temptation, do the best you can on your test, and make sure to study next time.

However, if you are not convinced of this, you will face great conflict. You will want to do what you believe is right, but the longer you lean on your own understanding and entertain all the "logic" that the Enemy has given you, the more likely it is that you will become convinced that cheating is the best option.

As the original deception tightens its grip, your frustration with the moral dilemma you are in often gets turned toward God: Why has God asked you to make a decision that you now believe will lead to your harm? You have long forgotten the fact that you are in this situation because you chose not to study, not because God's instructions are somehow flawed. With your trust in God's good intentions undermined, you take matters into your own hands and decide for yourself what is best for you. And so you cheat.

Every decision we make builds momentum, either for good or for evil.

Now you may be thinking, *I **know** cheating is wrong, but in that particular situation, if I had to choose between summer school and a little cheating one time, it would probably be better to just go ahead and cheat.* This is a perfect example of why we must never lean on our own understanding. Most of the time we can't see down the road far enough to know what kind of consequence this sin will cause—not just in this one situation, but for the rest of your life.

Let's say you cheated, passed the class, and never got caught. If you isolate that one situation, it may seem like the sin of cheating was worth it. The problem is that no choice is ever isolated. Every decision we make sets up patterns in our lives and conditions us for future actions.

We all want to believe that we will make the right choice every *other* time after we sin, but life simply doesn't work that way. Every decision we make builds momentum, either for good or for evil. When we give in once, it is much easier to give in a second time—and even easier the time after that. There are many rapists in jail right now who confess that everything started with a small look at pornography. Many drug addicts started by getting high "just this one time." And many who ended up having an affair first cheated on something small, like a test. In each scenario I'm sure that the initial sin seemed harmless at the time, and they didn't intend for things to progress. But that is how the Enemy works.

I once heard a saying that captures the truth of this: "Sin takes you further than you wanted to go, keeps you longer than you wanted to stay, and costs you more than you wanted to pay."

If our perspective is right from the beginning, we will never get to the point where we are reasoning with Satan.

This is why it is absolutely crucial that we identify the original deception and deal with it *before* it leads us down the wrong path. When the original deception is present in your life, you will constantly be lured into the battle of trying to weigh each decision between sin and obedience based on the benefits you can logically discern in the moment. This will consistently lead to sin because only God can see the full picture, and the Enemy's arguments will always sound convincing in the moment.

Instead, we must prevent the battle altogether. We do this by being fully convinced that God loves us and wants the best for us. Once we are convinced of this, it generates the necessary faith to enable us to trust Him and follow His instructions even when they seem difficult or don't make sense.

Consider the example of cheating on a test. Even though the Enemy made a convincing argument to cheat, if we are convinced of God's good intentions, *we won't even weigh the argument*. If our perspective is right from the beginning, we will never get to the point where we are reasoning with Satan. Instead, we reject his argument right away because even when we don't understand why God is asking us to do something or we don't know how things will turn out, we choose to believe in His character and trust that He always knows and wants what is best for us.

Is It in You?

Have you fallen prey to the original deception?

Are you holding back certain areas of your life from God because you are afraid of what will happen if you surrender them to Him? Do you feel that obeying God's instructions will be less fun than sinning? Do you sometimes question whether God is just trying to keep you from having a good time? Are there certain areas of your life in which you are convinced that obeying God will not work out for the best? Do you have areas of sin in your life from which—no matter how hard you try—you just can't seem to break free?

A yes to any of these questions indicates that the original deception is lurking inside of you. Maybe you have seen it play out a few times in your life; maybe you are seeing it play out many times each day. Whatever the case, resist the urge to be discouraged. It's just like the Enemy to deceive you into sin and then beat you up with guilt afterward.

Rather, if you are starting to see the original deception at work inside you, now is the time to be excited! As long as something is hidden from you, you can't fix it. However, once God shows you something, you can bring it into the light and begin to deal with it. Imagine how much easier your life-choices will be without the original deception!

Remember, the Enemy has no new tricks. If we can learn to overcome the original deception, we will be on the path to greater obedience to God and the blessings that follow. In the next chapters, we'll bulk ourselves up with some scriptural muscles that will let us kick the original deception out of our lives once and for all.

Questions

1. How has the original deception been at work in your life?

2. Is your first response to temptation to trust God, or doubt His instructions?

3. Do you have any areas in your life that you have consistently withheld from God? If so, why? Are *your* choices in that area working out for the best? Does your answer sound like truth or deception?

4. Knowing that God always has your best interest in mind, why do you think you fear trusting certain areas of your life to His control?

5. What are some ways that you can begin to resist the original deception?

chapter 7

principles for success

Perhaps at this point you are thinking, *I don't believe the original deception is my problem. I trust God. My problem is that even though I know God is for me and sin will work out badly for me, I sin anyway!* If this describes you, believe it or not, the original deception is still the cause of your problem.

The reason it seems harder to recognize is because we often confuse knowing and believing. The fact that you *know* in your mind that Jesus loves you and that He can be trusted doesn't mean you really *believe* that. The truest evidence of what you believe is found in your actions, not your mind.

For example, if a man tells his wife he loves her but then is abusive and treats her horribly, does he really love her? What if someone confronted him about the way he was treating her and he said, "No, you don't understand—I really love her"? Would that make it true? Even if he really thinks he loves her, he is deceived. Real love is proven by actions, not by words or even emotions.

> **The truest evidence of what you believe is found in your actions, not your mind.**

The same is true when it comes to sin. Often the original deception flies under the radar in our lives because we think, *I already know God loves me. I've sung the song since I was a kid—"Jesus loves me this I know, for the Bible tells me so."* It may be true that we know this in our minds, but do we believe it in our hearts to such a degree that it determines our actions? Until the truth of God's character becomes a deep-rooted belief, the original deception will continue to wreak havoc in our lives.

When we sin consistently in an area, it reveals that deep down inside we believe—perhaps unconsciously—that the sin will benefit us more than obeying God. Consistent sin always serves as evidence that the original deception is present, lurking somewhere behind our sinful actions.

So how do we rid ourselves of the original deception once and for all? Romans 12:2 gives us a key. The first part of the verse says, "Don't copy the behavior and customs of this world, but let God transform you into a new person by changing the way you think" (NLT).

**If we want to change our
actions, we have to get rid of the
deception that is causing them.**

When our minds are tainted by the original deception, we
end up copying the behaviors and customs of this world,
which tell us to do whatever seems right to us at the moment—
and we know the dark roads such decisions lead us down.

However, Romans 12:2 tells us that if we let *God* change
the way we think and believe, we will be transformed into a
new person. Again, what we believe deeply determines our
actions, so when our minds are clouded by any type of deception, our actions will always follow that deception—whether
we want them to or not! But the opposite is also true. If we can
enthrone truth in place of that deception, our actions will
follow the truth instead. This is why the Bible tells us we can
be transformed by changing the way we think.

Imagine a boy who thinks the word "stupid" is spelled
s-t-o-o-p-i-d. Because of his belief, every time he needs to
spell that word he will get it wrong. However, if someone
shows him that the actual way to spell the word is s-t-u-p-i-d,
then from that moment his actions—spelling the word—will
be transformed. If we want to change our actions, we have to
get rid of the deception that is causing them.

Let's look at a few simple truths and see if we can expose
this original deception for the lie that it is and break its power
once and for all.

The Character Principle

Many people say that they want to obey God, but when something really tempting comes along, even though they know it disagrees with His Word, the sin just seems too difficult to pass up. When we are dazzled by a certain temptation, it can be hard to think clearly because we're too focused on the specifics of the sin. *Is this sin wrong all the time? Will a little sin really hurt me? Will I get caught?*

The *character* of the person behind the thought or temptation is more important than *what* is being presented.

Instead, it is much more helpful to go back a step in the process and look at *who* the thought is coming from. Let's call this the "character principle." The character principle tells us that the *character* of the person behind the thought or temptation is more important than *what* is being presented.

Whenever we are tempted, there will be two voices speaking into our lives—the Enemy and the Lord. The Enemy hopes to lead us into sin, and the Lord hopes to lead us into life. Trying to analyze every thought in the moment of temptation can be overwhelming and confusing. However, if we learn to look at the *character* of the one presenting the thought, and less at the thought itself, it is easier to stay on track.

Let's look at a few Scriptures that reveal to us the character of both God and Satan. These verses will help us focus more on the *who* of our temptations, and less on the *what*. First let's just look at a few verses of what the Bible tells us about God:

- "I came that they may have life, and have it abundantly." (John 10:10 NASB)
- "Greater love has no one than this, that he lay down his life for his friends." (John 15:13)
- "But when he, the Spirit of truth, comes, he will guide you into all truth." (John 16:13)

The picture of God's character is clear. First, He tells us plainly that His purpose is to give us an abundant life. Next, we see that He put actions behind His words by showing us the highest form of love that could ever be shown. He died in our place to make a way for us to experience the abundant life He promised for all eternity. Then to help us on our journey, He sent His Holy Spirit to be our guide every day of our lives. The Spirit guides us by continually comforting us and leading us into truth.

Every time the Enemy tries to convince us that sin is a good choice, there is a 100 percent chance he's lying.

God sounds like a pretty trustworthy person. So what is the character of the competing voice in our heads? Let's look at some truths about the Devil:

- "Stay alert! Watch out for your great enemy, the devil. He prowls around like a roaring lion, looking for someone to devour." (1 Peter 5:8 NLT)

- "The thief comes only to steal and kill and destroy." (John 10:10 NASB)

- "You belong to your father, the devil, and you want to carry out your father's desire. He was a murderer from the beginning, not holding to the truth, for there is no truth in him. When he lies, he speaks his native language, for he is a liar and the father of lies." (John 8:44)

The picture of our Enemy stands in stark contrast to the picture of God. In the first verse we see that he is like a roaring lion, prowling around and waiting for the perfect moment to devour us with his deception. Next, we see that the goals of his attacks are to steal, kill, and destroy. Finally, we are told that Satan is the "father of lies." He may be whispering in your ear that following his temptation will bring you pleasure or that following God's ways will be boring, but this Scripture promises us that his words are *always* a lie. In fact, the verse goes as far as to say, "There is no truth in him." This means that every time the Enemy tries to convince us that sin is a good choice, there is a 100 percent chance he's lying.

A faithful Savior who always speaks the truth, or a treacherous beast who always lies? When we focus on their character, it becomes much easier to decide who to follow.

Any thought that comes from the Enemy, no matter how good it seems, is a lie meant to destroy us. That is simply Satan's character. On the other hand, any thought that comes from God, no matter how hard it may seem to follow, is truth that will lead us to a more abundant life. That is simply God's character.

Think about it this way. Imagine if a good friend invited you to go with them on a tropical vacation to a secluded, private island in the Caribbean. They offered to fly you over in their private jet to enjoy a week of fun, sand, sun, and luxury accommodations. I think it would be safe to assume you would have a strong desire to go. However, let's say someone invites you on an even *cooler* (if that were possible) trip to an island—only you know this person happens to be a mass murderer. How motivated would you be to go? No matter how much "fun" they promised you would have on that secluded island, you wouldn't even consider it.

> **In moral issues, if something
> is harmful in large doses,
> it is usually harmful
> in smaller doses, too.**

It's no different with the choices we make each day. Satan is the ultimate mass murderer. Think about all the deaths that have resulted from people following his temptation into drugs, alcohol addiction, violence, and other sin. He desires to do the same to you. But Satan isn't stupid. He knows that if we consciously pick between a lying murderer and a faithful friend, he'll fail at tempting us every time. So he lies. He tries to make sin seem like fun or necessary to our happiness. Every time he tempts us, he dresses up his evil plans as good choices— choices that will be even *better* than what God plans for us.

This is why the character principle is vital. No matter how great the temptations of the Enemy may seem, we know the truth about him: he is a liar, a thief, and a killer. We can reject every temptation that comes from him—not by sorting out all the particulars of that opportunity to sin, but by looking at his character. Trusting the devil is, to be honest, about as s-t-o-o-p-i-d as we can get.

The Extreme Principle

Another tool to help us see through the deception of the Enemy is the "extreme principle." The extreme principle is the process of magnifying something in order to make it clearer. Sometimes if we focus only on the one situation right in front of us, it can be easier to be deceived. But if we push the situation to its extreme and walk down the road a ways in our mind, it often becomes much easier to see whether that choice will prove beneficial or harmful. In moral issues, if something is harmful in large doses, it is usually harmful in smaller doses, too.

For example, the Enemy may say something like, "Come on, just get drunk this one time. Everyone is doing it. It's no big deal, and besides, it's going to be so much fun." It should be fairly clear that drunkenness is sin, since it is against the law to drink if you are underage and the Bible warns us against intoxication no matter how old you are (Ephesians 5:18). However, if we get lured into weighing our decision based only on that one situation, we may be more likely to buy into the Enemy's "It won't be a big deal, just this once" sales pitch. To make the situation easier to discern, simply take it to the extreme. Let's say you *really* go for it with getting drunk. I mean, you go extreme and drink as much as you possibly can. Would it really prove to be tons of fun? Would it lead to a happier life? Of course not! You have a better chance of becoming an alcoholic, living in a van down by the river. When you take it to the extreme, it becomes much clearer.

Perhaps you are tempted to get high and the Enemy whispers, "Oh, it will be so much fun. You'll love it, and you can leave all your problems behind." Take it to the extreme and see if it proves true. Let's say you got high as much as you could—you really dove in headfirst. Would all your problems go away? No way! You have a better chance of ending up in prison with a 400-pound roommate named Brutus. Not good.

The Enemy is always tempting you with one objective in mind: to steal, kill, and destroy.

Or maybe the Enemy reasons, "Come on, just have sex. Everyone is doing it. It will make you so happy. Just look at the movies. Everything always works out in the end." Again, take it to the extreme, and see if you can see through the lie. If the simple act of sex itself really produced happiness, then prostitutes would be the happiest people on earth. Obviously I'm being a little sarcastic here, but I think you can see how the extreme principle can help you see through Satan's lies.

You can apply this principle to any area of temptation you are wrestling with. Just take it to the extreme, and it will become much clearer how to handle that individual situation.

Perhaps you are thinking, *Sure, those things look bad if you take them to the extreme. But I'm not going to get drunk (or whatever the sin may be) that much—just a couple of times—so the extreme principle doesn't apply to my situation.* Remember that the purpose of the extreme principle is simply to reveal more clearly whether or not the behavior is harmful. If we realize that it is sin, we must understand that even one step down that road will have negative consequences. I'll say it again: When it comes to moral issues, if something is harmful in a large dose, it's not good for you in small doses either. If a lot of drunkenness is bad, a little isn't good for you either. So it doesn't matter if it's just a "little" sin—it's still going to harm you.

The bottom line is that sin will never deliver what it promises.

One of the Enemy's favorite traps is to get you to believe that you can control the situation and stop walking down the road of sin whenever you want. As much as we would like to believe this, it is simply not the case. Often it takes only one time to bring destruction into your life. I can't tell you how many people I have heard of who had sex only once and got an STD or climbed in a car with a drunk person only once and are now dead. The Enemy is always tempting you with one objective in mind: to steal, kill, and destroy.

We can test God's commands with the extreme principle, too. For example, the Bible tells us to have sex only with the person to whom we are married. Let's take this command to the extreme: What if everyone had sex with only the person to whom they were married? Do you know that all sexually transmitted diseases would be wiped off the face of the earth in one generation? Most of the unwanted pregnancies that lead to abortions would be avoided. Our world is scrambling for a cure for AIDS. They tell us there is no cure—but there *is* a cure. If everyone followed the instructions in God's Word, there would be no AIDS!

We could go on and on. God tells us to love one another. If we all took that to the extreme, can you imagine the results? No more war. No more crime. No more hate. What a transformed world we would be living in!

When we take things to their extreme, it becomes much easier to see both the Enemy's deception and God's truth. The bottom line is that sin will never deliver what it promises. It promises fun and joy and fulfillment, but in the end it will always steal, kill, and destroy.

This might sound kind of gross, but when speaking about sin I have often used the line, "Sin is like chocolate-covered feces." Seriously! When you look at it from a distance, it looks like chocolate. You pick it up, and it feels like chocolate. You bring it closer, and it even smells like chocolate. You take a little nibble on the outer chocolate covering, and it even tastes like chocolate. But once you dive in, you are in for a big surprise. It's not at all what you were expecting! Satan is *always* going to package sin to make it look good. But when you dive in, it is never what you were hoping for.

This is a truth I have seen play out time and time again in my own life and the lives of many others. For example, when I was in high school I was so convinced that a life of popularity would be worth whatever compromise was necessary. It looked great at the onset. But once I dove in, it resulted in bondage, brokenness, and addiction that nearly destroyed my life.

Don't Jump

Beyond the character principle and the extreme principle, there are certain spiritual laws we need to consider. Just as natural laws like the law of gravity govern our universe, spiritual laws govern our lives. No one would stand at the top of a bridge and say, "I know about the law of gravity, but I am going to jump because *this* time I think I'll float in midair!" We would never do that because we know the law of gravity applies *every single time.*

It is the same with spiritual laws. Consider sexual immorality. God created sex for marriage, and in that context it is a wonderful thing. However, outside of marriage, sex can be destructive to our hearts and lives. The Enemy realizes that because sex will almost always give an initial feeling of pleasure, it is a perfect area for him to tempt us. He knows that we will often be so caught up in the momentary pleasure that we will fail to see the long-term consequences.

We all know people who have been tempted to "jump off

the bridge" of sexual immorality. Perhaps they even know it's wrong. But because of the original deception in their lives, they think it will be worth it somehow. So they jump, and just like jumping off a real bridge there is an initial rush. The whole way down they may say things like, "Look at me, I'm so free! I'm having so much fun! This feels *so* good! You're really missing out!" Each phrase gets a little fainter as they get closer to the ground.

But eventually sin will always bring destructive consequences.

Then, just like jumping off a real bridge, eventually they hit the ground. *BAM!* The spiritual law proves true. A boyfriend breaks up with you and breaks your heart. You have lasting feelings of guilt about how you treated your girlfriend. You regret giving yourself away. You're pregnant, or you get someone pregnant, or you contract a sexually transmitted disease. Just like the law of gravity, sin will take you down *every single time.*

Nowhere to Run

We can all think of times when, because of the original deception, we gave in to sin and learned the hard way that it wasn't worth it. We can also think of times when we gave in to sin and it seemed like a lot of fun—and we can't even think of any consequences. This is another trap of the Enemy.

Sometimes he will try to keep us from feeling the consequences of our actions to lure us deeper into sin.

Even though we may not be able to see them right away, the truth is that there are always consequences to sin. Sometimes they are immediate, while other times they lag behind. But eventually sin will always bring destructive consequences.

Sometimes we sin and think, *Nothing happened.* As a result, we continue walking down the wrong road. This leads to further sin. In some cases, things may still seem okay for quite some time, but eventually we make a certain decision and end up paying for everything—big-time. Only then do we realize the price of all the sins that led us to that point.

The danger is that by the time we realize our error, we are often so far down the road that we are in big trouble. In those moments we ask questions like, "How did I get here? How did this happen?" What happened is that we finally experienced the consequences of that first bad decision that we thought we got away with. All of those seemingly small and harmless decisions led us down a road that ends in pain and regret.

Whether they are immediate or delayed, sin will always produce horrible consequences in our lives.

Sin = Insane!

Sin, by definition, is insane. One of the definitions of insanity is doing the same thing over and over and expecting a different result.

So often this is exactly our mentality when we sin. We jump off the bridge in some area of sin, hit the ground, and realize that the price wasn't worth it. But when we get tempted again, instead of learning our lesson, we go right back up to the same bridge (or another one) and jump into sin again, thinking, *Maybe* this *time it will work out.* That's crazy. The more we jump and hit the ground, the more broken our lives become—and soon we are messed up and hurting. Our brokenness and pain makes following Jesus harder and robs us of the experiences God has for us.

Utilizing the extreme principle and the character principle will help you see clearly in the moment of temptation and keep you from being lured off the bridge. You can further protect yourself by finding your own Scriptures about things like the character of God, the character of our Enemy, the goodness of God, and the pitfalls of sin. Allow God and His Word to permanently change what you believe to be true—and that true belief will guide your actions.

However, to overcome the original deception once and for all we must continue right to the heart of the deception and replace it with truth. We learned that the main goal of the original deception is to destroy trust, and that our ability to trust is rooted in what we believe to be true about God's character. To deliver the death blow to the original deception, we must focus on what allows it to thrive—the inaccurate way we see God, which is the subject we'll consider in the next chapter.

Questions

1. Can you think of a time when you willingly sinned and the results were worth it? Do you think you'll still be able to say that years from now?

2. If your answer to question 1 is "no," then why would you ever expect sin to be worth it in the future?

3. How can you practically apply the character principle in your fight against sin?

4. How can you practically apply the extreme principle in your fight against sin?

5. Romans 12:2 says that we can transform our actions by changing the way we think. What are some ways you can begin to change the way you think about God's instructions? How do you think about God's instructions now?

chapter 8

God's character unveiled

I want to ask you a simple but extremely important question: *How do you see God?*

Try to avoid just giving the Sunday school answer. Really think about it. If you're not careful, you'll just reply that God is love or Savior or friend or some other cliché that you have heard throughout the years. But the question isn't what you have *heard* is true or what you *think* you should believe. The question is what you *actually* believe. Think about it.

The reason for this question should be clear by this point: The way you see God determines how you will act. If you want to change your response to temptation and sin, you must first change your perception of God.

The rest of this section contains many questions that cut to the heart of how you see God. This isn't information that you need to learn. Rather, each question is a chance for you to slow down and be honest with God. Read the next few pages slowly. Open your heart. Let these questions help you develop a better understanding of the way you view God.

If you want to change your response to temptation and sin, you must first change your perception of God.

Do you see God as someone whose instructions will only steal your fun and end up making your life boring? Or do you see Him as someone whose instructions are meant to lead you to the fullest, most fulfilling life possible (John 10:10)?

Have you imagined God as someone who is not very interested in your life? Or do you see Him as one who is so concerned with you that His thoughts about *you* outnumber the grains of sand on the seashore (Psalm 139:17–18)?

Do you think that God is always mad at you or waiting to "slam" you the first chance He gets? Or do you know God to be someone who is slow to anger and full of patience, kindness, and forgiveness (Psalm 145:8)?

Have you been deceived into believing that God has written you off because of your past? Or do you see Him like a loving father who, no matter what you have done, waits for you to return to Him so that He can heal and restore you (Luke 15:20–24)?

**God is exceedingly
interested in you.**

Do you picture God as being unconcerned about your feelings? Or did you know that He cares so deeply about your concerns that He sees your tears and records each one (Psalm 56:8 NLT)?

When you imagine God, is He someone who is unapproachable and distant? Or do you see Him as someone who wants you to share your concerns with Him because He cares for you (1 Peter 5:7)?

Do you see God as one who cares about you in a general, non-emotional sense? Or do you see Jesus as the one who, after giving His life for you, sits day and night before the throne of God the Father to pray for you (Hebrews 7:25)?

Who God *Really* Is

Regardless of what you may have thought, God is not some disinterested being who has given you instructions to follow but doesn't care about your happiness and quality of life along the way. God is exceedingly interested in you. He cares about you more deeply than you could ever understand— He cares about your thoughts, your emotions, your future, your hurts, your pains. He cares about your freedom and your future. Did you know that before you were born He knew you and designed a beautiful plan for your life? It is a plan that will honor Him while leading you to great fulfillment and joy. The Bible says that God knit you together in your mother's womb

(Psalm 139:13). He created you perfectly for the life He has planned for you. When you were born, He rejoiced at the opportunity to get to know you. He wants to guide you to things so great that the Bible tells us, "No eye has seen, no ear has heard, no mind has conceived what God has prepared for those who love him" (1 Corinthians 2:9).

But as you walk through this life, there is an Enemy who is filled with hate, and he desperately wants to destroy your life. He is always tempting, always prowling around trying to find ways, both big and small, to get you off course. He exists to steal, kill, and destroy.

God, however, in His great love for you, wants to protect you from harm. You are His prized creation. In His love He instructs you not to follow the deceptions of the Enemy. He gives you His Word, He gives you the Holy Spirit, and He continues to pray for you day and night. When you hurt, He hurts. When you fall, He picks you up. When you sin, He forgives you. And even when you turn your back on Him, He is always waiting, longing for you to return to Him like the father of the prodigal son (see Luke 15).

It is literally impossible for God to love you any more than He does right now.

This is the wonderful truth of who God really is. Perhaps you are one whom the Enemy has successfully made to feel worthless; perhaps you can scarcely imagine a perfect God loving you perfectly *as you are right now.*

But this is the reality of God. It doesn't matter what anyone else says or thinks about you. It doesn't even matter what *you* think about you. The truth is that God loves you perfectly and eternally. It is literally impossible for God to love you any more than He does right now.

Perfectly Loved

God's love is not conditional. It does not change based on your performance, past history, or social standing. God loves you with the same love that He had for His Son, Jesus Christ. I want you to see that perfect, unchanging love with your own eyes.

John 17 records the moments just before Jesus is betrayed and handed over to the Roman government to be crucified. Immediately before He is arrested, Jesus uses His last few minutes to pray for His disciples. In John 17:20–23, He makes it clear that He is not just praying for those who are with Him but for all who will ever believe in Him. Then in the last part of verse 23, Jesus asks the Father that, through what He is about to do on the cross, we would be able to experience such unity with the Father "that the world will know that you sent me and that you love them as much as you love me" (NLT).

Did you catch that? *God loves you as much as He loves His only Son.* Take a second to let that sink in. It's easy for us to understand that God the Father loved Jesus. Jesus was called God's only begotten Son, and He perfectly obeyed everything the Father asked. Yet God loves you just as much. It is as unbelievable as it is true. Here's another incredible fact: since God loves you perfectly, He can never love anything more than He loves you. You may want to pause for a moment to meditate on that truth and consider what it means for you. In fact, I would encourage you to meditate on it as much as is necessary for this truth to sink deep into you heart.

Of course, the Enemy will try to convince you that God can't love you, or that you're not worthy of His love, but none of that changes God's perfect love for you. God has declared His love for you in His unchanging Word and proved it by sending Jesus. You simply need to make the choice to believe it.

If you realize that you don't really see God as a loving Father whose every instruction is designed to bring you life, you must immediately begin to proactively change the way you think, and the best way to do that is by immersing yourself in God's living Word. God's Word is not an ordinary book. God has anointed the Bible to transform our thoughts, beliefs, and actions as we read it. As you meditate on Scriptures related to God's character, your beliefs will begin to change for the better. This transformation will take time, so I encourage you to begin right away—perhaps by reading and rereading the Scriptures at the end of this chapter.

The Key to Everything

In previous chapters we learned that the character of God is perfectly good. Like a loving father, He always desires what is best for us. Taking this truth from mere knowledge to firm belief is the key to experiencing God. That truth will cause us to trust and obey Him when He asks us to do something, even if we don't understand why. When we live consistently in this manner, we will experience God in ways we never dreamed possible.

Let me give you an illustration. The president of the United States is guarded by the Secret Service. These agents are so dedicated to the president's well-being that they have pledged to protect him even at the cost of their own lives. Let's imagine that the president has just finished a day that was so busy he had not yet had time to eat. Fortunately for him, he happens to be finishing his day in the city of his favorite restaurant. He mentions it to the Secret Service agents and they immediately make arrangements. The president arrives at the restaurant, and when the food is served, the thought goes through his mind, *I can't think of anything in the world I desire more than to eat this meal.* Just as he is about to take his first bite, the Secret Service agents swarm in and say, "Mr. President, we have to move you right now!" We all know that without a second thought he would get up immediately and leave the dinner behind. Why? Because he trusts their intentions. Even in the face of something extremely desirable, it never even crosses his mind not to obey their instructions.

Only when you see God as someone whose every instruction is intended to protect you, will you too be able to consistently walk away from temptation without question. When you truly trust God, you will be able to follow Him even when you don't understand why. Think about it. If the president will respond with such trust to Secret Service agents who have only *pledged* to protect him with their lives, how much more should we give our trust to a God who has *already given* His life for us?

Our ability to progress and grow in our Christian life will

always stem from developing a love relationship with God that produces trust and, as a result, surrender.

It may seem like a simple concept, but let me show you why a transformed view of God is the key to a deeper experience with God. Most of us try to fight sin in our own strength, which results in what I call the *sin cycle*. It looks something like this: You realize you have an area of sin in your life and you want to change. So you try really hard to do better and perhaps you make it two weeks without falling in that particular area—and then you fall. This is often followed by feelings of guilt and condemnation. After you pick yourself up, you decide to try again, but this time you try even harder and maybe make it three weeks before slipping up. Again, you go through the frustration of failing and start the process all over again. This process of trying to change in your own strength only to fail again becomes a cycle that eventually causes most to either give up or justify why keeping the sin is okay after all.

However, when your view of God changes and you begin to see His loving intentions for what they are, a whole new process begins. The more you grasp of God's love for you, the more you will find your natural response to that love will be to love Him back. First John 4:19 says, "We love because He first loved us." Only when we truly realize His love for us can this response of love for Him begin to grow in our hearts. But once it does, everything changes. When we grasp God's love and respond by loving Him back, our next response will be to begin drawing near to Him. The fear and uncertainty we felt about God's intentions when the original deception was present is now replaced with trust because we see His true character. As this transformed view of God frees us to draw near, that's when the real miracle happens—God begins to transform you into a completely different person. Second Corinthians 3:18 reminds us that as we draw near to the Lord in relationship that we will actually be transformed into His likeness.

Here's why this is such a game changer. The sin cycle is doomed to failure because even though your intentions are good, essentially you are trying to conquer sin in your own strength. Long term, this will always result in failure. If we could overcome sin in our own power, Jesus would never have needed to come and die for us. The truth is, we can't conquer sin on our own. We need His power to transform us and this is exactly what happens as we begin to understand His love and draw near in relationship. Philippians 2:13 says, "For God is working in you, giving you the desire and the power to do what pleases him" (NLT). Did you catch that? God is able to transform you to such a degree that not only will you have the power to obey Him—you'll have the desire, too. If you've ever been locked in the sin cycle, this is great news! Sometimes people ask me if it is still hard to resist getting high because of my past. In all honesty it is not hard for me at all. You couldn't pay me to get high because I don't want to anymore. God has completely transformed my desires to where I simply don't desire to sin in that way.

When you try to conquer sin in your own strength, it will always result in the sin cycle because you are trying to act against your nature. But when you draw near to Christ in love, His power begins to transform you and gives you a new nature. When this new nature takes hold in an area of your life, obedience begins to be a natural outcome.

Imagine you had a fruit tree that was producing fruit that you didn't like and you wanted to stop the tree from producing this fruit. There are two options you could pursue to accomplish this. Your first option is to simply pick all the fruit off of the tree. The problem with this approach is that it's only a temporary solution. It's only a matter of time until that fruit will return. The other option you have is to cut the tree down at the roots and plant a different one. Only then can you be assured that the problem has been solved once and for all.

But we must understand that everything starts with grasping God's true character and His loving intentions.

It's the same with our lives. When you try to conquer sin in your own strength, it has the same effectiveness as picking the fruit off of the tree. There may be some temporary results, but it's only a matter of time until the sin returns because we haven't been changed. We simply addressed our behavior without dealing with the root of that behavior. To see permanent change in our lives, we must address the root of our behavior, which is our heart. When we draw near to the Lord in relationship, He actually changes our hearts. When our hearts (the roots) have been changed, our actions (the fruit) will permanently change as well.

Watch how different these results are from the sin cycle.

We first grasp God's love for us, which expels the original deception. With the original deception removed, we are able to trust Him and draw near to Him in love. As our relationship grows, His grace and power transforms us and we become more like Him. This of course leads to greater obedience, which leads to a deeper relationship. And the cycle just continues. The more we actually experience God, the more we see His love; the more we see His love, the more we love Him; the more we love Him, the more we draw near; the more we draw near, the more we are transformed and empowered; the more we are empowered, the more we are able to obey, and on and on. Now we see a whole new cycle resulting in permanent transformation and increased experience with God instead of the frustrating failure that the sin cycle brings.

While it is true that as long as we are on earth there will always be a certain level of struggle with sin, really seeing God for who He is will begin a process that will empower you to obey Him, and as a result, experience Him on a whole new level. But we must understand that everything starts with grasping God's true character and His loving intentions.

What a Difference the Truth Makes

Take a moment to consider the difference that breaking the original deception will make in your life. Perhaps right now you want to obey God, but you are fearful of how it will turn out. First John 4:18 says, "There is no fear in love. But perfect love drives out fear, because fear has to do with punishment. The one who fears is not made perfect in love." When you begin to really understand God's perfect love, it drives out any fear associated with giving Jesus the keys to your life. Conversely, if you continue to fear, it is a sign that the truth of God's love has yet to penetrate your heart to the depth that is necessary to eliminate your fear and apprehension.

Can you imagine what it would be like to live a life where you are free to surrender the most important areas of your life to God without fear? Can you imagine what it would be like to conquer some of your sins so completely that even your *desire* for that sin dissolves? This is the type of victory God wants to bring in your life! (Remember Philippians 2:13.) God's design is for you to be so completely transformed that you obey, not because you have to, but because you want to!

Jesus gives us a great illustration of this in Matthew 13:44. "The kingdom of heaven is like treasure hidden in a field. When a man found it, he hid it again, and then in his joy went and sold all he had and bought that field." In this verse, the man gives up *everything* he has to purchase the field with the treasure— but he actually *rejoices* to do so because he knows what he is getting is so much better than what he is giving up.

It is the same with us. When we realize what a treasure it is to be able to experience more of God and follow His leadership to abundant life, we too will joyfully part with whatever is necessary to continue following Him. Jesus never intended following Him to be a drag, where we constantly feel like we have to do things we don't want to do. If it appears this way, it is because we have bought into the original deception. Jesus' desire is that walking with Him will be a joyful process of following someone we love in response to His great love for us.

Do You Have
the Right God?

When I was getting ready to marry my wife, Alicia, I heard all the warnings from my friends. "Mike, are you sure you want to do this? You probably won't be able to stay out all hours with the fellas as much as you do now. You'll have to act more civilized in public and, worst of all, she'll probably make you put the toilet seat down! Are you sure you're up for this?"

The truth, however, is that the treasure is always worth the sacrifice!

I promise you, I was so in love that when I heard these things, I just looked at them and said, "Are you kidding me? Who cares!" I knew the treasure I was getting in Alicia was so much more valuable than anything I would need to part with to have her. In fact, I was actually excited to make any changes necessary for our love to flourish. That is what love is supposed to be like, whether with your future spouse or with God.

When the time comes for you to get married, your single friends may warn you about some of the same small sacrifices. If they start warning you about petty things like putting the toilet seat down and you find yourself thinking, *Well, I don't know if he or she is worth all that!* trust me, you have got the wrong person! When you find the right one, you will be excited to alter your life in any way necessary to successfully join lives with your future spouse. In the same way, if you are constantly thinking, *Boy, it is such a drag to follow Jesus. I can't believe all I have to sacrifice to be a Christian,* trust me that you have the wrong God! You are not seeing Him for who He really is. When you do, you will realize—just like meeting the girl or guy of your dreams—whatever you need to give up will pale in comparison to what you receive.

In the Christian life, there is sacrifice involved. Certain things must die, but it is death for the sake of life! Leaving the sin that holds us back allows us to freely obtain the treasure of God's promises. Don't be fooled! When God asks you to lay something down, the Enemy will immediately try to convince you that God is cruel. The truth, however, is that the treasure is always worth the sacrifice!

It's a Process

Ridding ourselves of the original deception will be a continuous battle, and it will take time. You may make a lot of progress at first, and then later realize there are still a few areas in which you are fighting the desire to give in to sin. This is normal. Some deceptions are so deeply rooted in us that it takes time for God's truth to penetrate the hardened layers of deception and remove them. The key is to avoid discouragement. The Enemy will resist you every step of the way and tell you that you will never change. Don't believe it—you will.

In my life there have been some temptations that were easily dealt with and others that took years. But if you keep going, God *will* change you over time. When you don't know what else to do, the Holy Spirit will be there to guide you. He will lead you to Scriptures that keep changing the way you think and act. To some extent we will always wrestle with sinful desires until Jesus comes back, but the more we are able to see God for who He really is, the easier the struggle becomes.

Take some time now to review the following Scriptures. Consider choosing several that speak to your heart and memorizing them. That way, in moments of temptation, they will be readily available to you to strike down the Enemy's deception.

- **"Are not two sparrows sold for a penny? Yet not one of them will fall to the ground apart from the will of your Father. And even the very hairs of your head are all numbered. So don't be afraid; you are worth more than many sparrows." (Matthew 10:29–31)**

At the time Jesus walked the earth, you could buy two sparrows for one penny! Jesus uses this example to show us how attentive He is to our lives. Not even one of those sparrows, which were considered of such little value, fell to the ground without God's awareness. In effect, God is saying, "If I am this attentive to and concerned about a sparrow, you have nothing to fear—I am *exponentially* more concerned about you. I am so concerned about you that I even keep track of the number of hairs on your head!"

- **"The world will know that you sent me and that you love them as much as you love me." (John 17:23 NLT)**

We discussed this verse earlier. To me, this is one of the most amazing verses in the Bible about God's love for us. To know that God looks at you with the same love and affection that He does His Son, Jesus, is an overwhelming thought.

- **"We know what real love is because Jesus gave up his life for us."** (1 John 3:16 NLT)

Jesus has already proved His love to us by suffering and dying in our place. Is there anything more that a person could ever do to prove their love? Surely after what He has done for us, it only makes sense that we would trust Him with our lives.

- **"Since he did not spare even his own Son but gave him up for us all, won't he also give us everything else?"** (Romans 8:32 NLT)

The revelation in this verse complements 1 John 3:16, which tells us that God has already proved His love. Then Romans 8:32 says, If God has already given up so much for us, will He really hold back on us now? There is no way God would go to the trouble of sacrificing His own Son for us if He were just going to abandon us later. If God went to such lengths already, surely we can trust Him in every other situation of our lives.

- **"How precious are your thoughts about me, O God. They cannot be numbered! I can't even count them; they outnumber the grains of sand! And when I wake up, you are still with me!"** (Psalm 139:17–18 NLT)

This verse can make us feel both safe and loved. Try to imagine how many grains of sand are on one beach. Now try to imagine all the grains of sand in the world—that's how many thoughts God thinks about you. So if you have ever doubted God's love or concern for you, you can put those doubts to rest once and for all. God thinks about you all the time! Every little thing you are going through matters to God and nothing slips past His attention.

- **"Because of the Lord's great love we are not consumed, for his compassions never fail. They are new every morning; great is your faithfulness."** (Lamentations 3:22–23)

God will never fail to look upon you with compassion. This word *compassions* literally means "tender love"—the same love a mother has for her child. God's tender love for you will never stop or fail. In fact, every morning He finds new ways to shower you with His love.

- **"Be strong and courageous. Do not be afraid or terrified because of them, for the Lord your God goes with you; he will never leave you nor forsake you."** (Deuteronomy 31:6)

God will never leave you nor forsake you. God promised this to the Israelites as they were about to enter the Promised Land. But in Hebrews 13:5 we are reminded that this is also a promise for us. Imagine: God will *never* leave or forsake you. Ever. Sometimes when bad things happen in our lives, we can feel like God has forsaken us, but this is simply not true. Even if you can't see His hand for a time or don't feel His presence, know that He has promised to always be with you and to never fail you.

- **"The Lord himself watches over you! The Lord stands beside you as your protective shade."** (Psalm 121:5 NLT)

What a vivid word picture to remind us that God is always there. On a bright, sunny day, you cannot escape your shadow. In the same way, God is always near you to watch over you and protect you.

- **"Even when I walk through the darkest valley, I will not be afraid, for you are close beside me."** (Psalm 23:4 NLT)

When we walk through "dark valleys of death," fear will always try to blind us so that we lose sight of God. This verse reminds us that even in the lowest moments of our lives we need not fear because God is still close beside us. Our circumstances may make it harder to see Him, but we need not fear because He *is* there.

- **"And I am convinced that nothing can ever separate us from God's love. Neither death nor life, neither angels nor demons, neither our fears for today nor our worries about tomorrow—not even the powers of hell can separate us from God's love."** (Romans 8:38 NLT)

What a powerful verse about God's love for us. Nothing can keep His love away from you—*nothing*! No matter what has happened in your past, what is happening in your present, or what happens in your future, God will always love you. Because He loves you, He will always be working for your best interest. And nothing in the universe will change that.

- **"'For I know the plans I have for you,' says the Lord, 'plans to prosper you and not to harm you, plans to give you hope and a future.'"** (Jeremiah 29:11)

In this verse God is very clear about His intentions for us. He wants to prosper us and give us hope and a future! Almost as if He knows that we may doubt Him, He reminds us, "My plans are not to harm you!" In other words, there is no evil in His character, only goodness. Whether you have walked the straight and narrow or struggled every step of the way, the Lord always has a plan that will give you hope and a future.

- **"The Lord directs the steps of the godly. He delights in every detail of their lives."** (Psalm 37:23 NLT)

So many times the Enemy deceives us into thinking that God doesn't care about us—or if He does, He only cares about the big things in our lives. When we believe this, we often feel like we are on our own when it comes to the smaller concerns that swarm our daily lives. But this verse puts that lie to rest once and for all. God delights in *every* detail of your life. Big or small, if it's important to you, it's important to God because He loves you!

- **"The Lord your God is with you, he is mighty to save. He will take great delight in you, he will quiet you with his love, he will rejoice over you with singing."** (Zephaniah 3:17)

There are two word pictures I love in this verse. Have you ever gotten so excited about something that you just broke out in song? This is how excited God gets about you. The second we mentioned in chapter 2. The love God gives is so strong it is able to quiet the cry of your heart.

- **"See how very much our Father loves us, for he calls us his children, and that is what we are!"** (1 John 3:1 NLT)

I love the analogy in this verse of a father and a child. So often we picture God as this big entity in the sky far removed from us. This couldn't be further from the truth.

As we have been discussing, God is near to us, concerned about us, and wants us to view Him like a loving, relatable father. After all, we really are His children!

- **"For as high as the heavens are above the earth, so great is his love for those who fear him." (Psalm 103:11)**

How high are the heavens above the earth? Immeasurably high, right? In the same way, God's love for those who fear Him cannot be measured. In the face of all the problems and temptations that we go through, it brings peace to know that God loves us in such an infinite way.

- **"Cast all your anxiety on him because he cares for you." (1 Peter 5:7)**

This verse shows us that we can bring God all the things that are troubling us—all our fears, needs, and concerns—because He really cares about them. It doesn't matter whether or not we *feel* His presence tangibly when we pour out our hearts to Him. We can be sure that He has heard us because, as this verse says, He cares for us.

- **"Take my yoke upon you and learn from me, for I am gentle and humble in heart, and you will find rest for your souls." (Matthew 11:29)**

When an animal is used to plow a field, a yoke is put on it so the person plowing the field can easily direct the animal. Jesus uses this analogy to help us understand the need to submit to His direction in our lives. But make sure you understand His heart here. He isn't asking this of you because He is on a power trip. Rather, out of His great love for you, He wants to lead your life in such a way that your soul will find rest.

- **" 'Though the mountains be shaken and the hills be removed, yet my unfailing love for you will not be shaken nor my covenant of peace be removed,' says the Lord, who has compassion on you."** (Isaiah 54:10)

In this verse, God is trying to paint a picture of the security of His love. He points to some of the strongest parts of visible creation and says, "Even if these were able to be shaken or removed, My love for you won't change. It is stronger and more permanent than the mountains and the hills."

If you continue to meditate on God's living Word, it will change you from the inside out.

- **"And he passed in front of Moses, proclaiming, 'The Lord, the Lord, the compassionate and gracious God, slow to anger, abounding in love and faithfulness.'"** (Exodus 34:6)

In this powerful verse, God Himself tells us what He is like! When Moses asks God to reveal Himself to him, this is how God introduces Himself. From His own mouth God says, "This is who I am! I am compassionate, gracious, slow to anger, and full of love and faithfulness." If we have flawed ideas about who God is, let this verse containing words from God's own mouth make His character completely clear.

- **"For God loved the world so much that he gave his one and only Son, so that everyone who believes in him will not perish but have eternal life."** (John 3:16 NLT)

The most famous verse in the Bible sums up everything we have been discussing. God loves us in such an unfathomable way that He chose to prove His love to us through His actions on the cross. The whole purpose of His loving action was to be good to us, that we might have eternal life.

These are just a few of the many verses in the Bible that reveal God's heart toward you. I pray that your view of God is already beginning to change. Dwell on these verses. Write them on cards and tape them to your dashboard. Slip them in your wallet. Pin them on your wall. If you continue to meditate on God's living Word, it will change you from the inside out.

Questions

1. Has your view of God changed after reading this chapter? How?

2. When you obey God, would you describe it more as a response of duty or love?

3. How does it make you feel to know that God can transform you so greatly that you will actually begin desiring to live the way He is instructing you (Philippians 2:13 NLT)? Have you experienced that level of transformation in your life yet? If so, in what area?

4. How can you begin to fuel your love for God so that the desire to obey Him will be increased in you?

5. Which two or three Scriptures from this chapter can you begin meditating on? Why do those verses seem important to you right now?

chapter 9

surrender stories

I have come to discover that trying to navigate through this life is a lot like walking through a minefield. Certain decisions may not look harmful on the surface, but when we step there, destruction is waiting. Jesus wants to help us navigate safely to the other side while the Enemy tries to lure us off course by convincing us that God's instructions are unnecessary and restrictive. With each step we must choose whom we will follow. When we trust God and follow His instructions, we will experience the fullness of life He promises. When we follow the Enemy's instructions, we will experience the destruction that sin brings. These are the parameters of life and there is no getting around them.

My own life testifies to these truths. Many times I ignored the Lord's warning and experienced the disastrous consequences.

I also experienced time and again the amazing blessings that followed when I responded to the Lord's instructions with obedience. Sometimes the consequences or benefits took years to see. But in the end, the Enemy always proved to be a liar, and God always proved to be faithful.

Even now you can begin your journey of deeper surrender that leads to a greater experience with God.

I want to share a few of my personal stories of surrender with you to help give you a clearer picture of what walking in surrender looks like in our everyday lives. As you read them, I encourage you to look for parallels in your own life where God may be speaking to you. Even now you can begin your journey of deeper surrender that leads to a greater experience with God.

Parting with Distractions

In chapter 4, I told the story of how I came to the point of total surrender in a movie theater one summer night when I was a teenager. Immediately after that, I began to seek the Lord as I never had before. I often stayed up late into the night praying and reading the Word. All through college, I continued to pursue the Lord with everything I had.

About the time I was getting ready to graduate, I began to

have a hunger to pursue ministry as a career. The problem was that the only opportunities available to me were in the business world, so I assumed that perhaps it wasn't the right time for ministry. However, on a mission trip the summer after I graduated college, the Lord opened the door for me to work for a large youth ministry and I jumped at the chance.

I loved it from the moment I arrived. There was such hunger for God in the atmosphere, and everyone seemed to have a passion to make a difference in the world. The fast-paced environment suited my personality—everywhere I turned there was another chance to minister or make a difference in the lives of others. All this opportunity also made it difficult to find balance. I felt like I could work 24/7 and still not get everything done. Eighty-hour work weeks weren't unusual, and when one ended I'd dive right into the next one.

After working there for six years, God began calling me to leave that role and start a ministry focused on traveling and speaking. As only God could do, He opened all the doors, and within one year's time I had transitioned to a full-time speaking ministry.

As you may imagine, my schedule changed immensely. While I still had a great deal of preparation to do, when I wasn't traveling my schedule was my own.

That was when little distractions began to clog my life. I was used to an environment with deadlines and accountability, but now I was my own boss and could set my own schedule. Even though I was diligent with the things I absolutely had to do, it was hard to keep distractions from devouring the rest of my time.

At first they seemed innocent enough. I thought, *As long*

as I am taking care of all the ministry necessities and spending adequate time with my family and with God, who cares what I do with the rest of my time?

This distraction got to the point that I stopped looking forward to going out of town for ministry.

The day the first major distraction entered my life, I had just finished a whirlwind month of ministry. I decided I would take a day to do absolutely nothing and simply unwind. A guy I know is a big video game buff, and he had been playing one of those online adventure games where you play with thousands of other people all over the world. When he recommended that I play with him for the day, it sounded like just the type of mindless activity I was hoping for. As I began to play, I discovered that the game had no end. The more you play your character, the higher levels you achieve, and there are endless opportunities to explore and discover *just one more thing*. There never seemed to be a good stopping point. I had so much fun playing that day that I figured I would play a little the next day, and the next . . . and the next.

Before long, I was devoting every spare second to playing this game—and even seconds I couldn't afford to spare. I stopped going to bed at the same time as my wife—a tradition we had—so I could play this dumb game. This distraction got to the point that I stopped looking forward to going out of town for ministry because I knew I wouldn't be able to play for several days! It all seems so stupid as I look back, but I was literally addicted to this game.

Lack of peace is one of the clearest ways I hear from God.

After a month or two, I realized it had become a problem. I tried to set boundaries for myself, but inevitably, I was right back online, telling myself I had earned a little break and would do just one more quest. Finally, one day I was praying to the Lord and I felt that He was asking me to give up the game—forever. Because of my state of mind at the time, this seemed like the least desirable thing the Lord could ask of me.

Instead of immediately surrendering and obeying, I began to wrestle with God in my mind. I offered up compromises to the Lord: "What if I just play a *couple of hours* per week?" But His conviction wouldn't lift. I continued to bargain. "Okay, God, what if I just played in the summer when I have a little more time, but not during the school year when I have a lot more to do?" His conviction remained. I must have offered up about fifteen alternative scenarios to quitting completely, but nothing I offered brought peace.

Lack of peace is one of the clearest ways I hear from God. Usually, when God convicts me of something, my sense of peace will be disturbed, telling me something is off course in my life. Most of the time, even if I don't want to admit it yet,

I already know the area that's causing the disturbance. In those moments it's imperative to go to God and get His guidance for the situation so you don't veer further off course.

However, sometimes I feel my peace lift and I am not yet sure of the cause. In those moments I will pray and ask God to reveal to me what is robbing me of peace. Once I have identified the area, I will again ask the Lord for guidance. As I think through which direction the Lord may be leading me, I will picture myself walking down different paths. As I "try out" each path in my mind, I am not looking for which solution seems the most logical, but rather which one restores peace. Sometimes a path that seems perfectly logical will still lack peace. Usually only one path will restore my sense of peace, and I know then what the Lord is asking of me.

As soon as I had a free second, I would feel anxious or discontent and rush to fill up that silence with a distraction.

Returning to my video game story, despite my very best sales pitches, I began to feel a very strong sense from the Lord that the only option that was going to be acceptable to Him was for me to never play this game again. I remember reasoning with Him that this was such a harsh decision—what if my circumstances changed later in life and I had more time to play? His conviction remained, and after two hours of wrestling with Him (unfortunately I can be stubborn), I realized there was no way out. Finally I spoke the words out loud: "God, I will never play that video game again." As soon as I said those words, the conviction lifted and peace returned. All the hold that this game had on me was instantly broken, and I rose up and left that room completely free. I never seriously entertained any attempts from the Enemy to make me rethink the decision. I can't say that freedom has always been so instant, but during my two-hour wrestling match I had plenty of time to come to terms with the decision before I made it. I knew if I decided to make the commitment to the Lord it would be final. Because I had settled the decision so completely in my mind the desire to play faded almost instantly.

After this experience, I began to feel the Lord telling me that I had to be extremely careful to avoid letting distractions into my life because He was doing something in me, and He needed my complete attention.

Unfortunately, for the next two years I seemed to always be struggling with at least one distraction that would rear its ugly head and steal my time and focus. At one point it was fantasy football, and then I thought about dabbling in real estate on the side. Next there was the stock market, and then it was getting consumed with the upcoming NFL draft. Each time I would get convicted and surrender the area. And each time, as soon as I became bored or discontented, instead of running to the Lord I would simply fall into a new distraction.

Eventually the Lord spoke to me and told me that I had been running so fast for so long that I had forgotten how to be still. As soon as I had a free second, I would feel anxious or discontent and rush to fill up that silence with a distraction. God began to tell me that if I would resist the desire to run to a distraction when I felt anxious, and if I would learn to run to Him instead, He would heal the cause of my anxiousness and lead me to a better life.

At first this was almost impossible for me to do. It was almost like I was addicted to constant stimulation and I had to go through withdrawals. The process was so uncomfortable that at times I became frustrated with God. I couldn't yet see why He was asking me to live this way. All I could see was my momentary discomfort.

However, as I continued to yield, the Lord began to reveal to me some unhealthy roots that were causing my subconscious need for constant action and distraction. He also began to change my desires so that I wanted to fill my free time with new, more meaningful things. In fact, not long after I finished my first draft of this book, the Lord spoke to me and said, "Mike, do you remember all the distractions I asked you to lay down? If you hadn't obeyed Me in those areas, you never would have written this book." Then He said, "And you never would have known you were *supposed* to. You would have been so caught up in those other things, it never would have occurred to you."

Instantly, it became clear to me why God had asked me to surrender my distractions to Him. He knew that my normal response to having free time was to immediatly fill it with a mindless activity. However, those activities were robbing me of the better things God had in store for me. He had plans for me to use my time for purposes that were much greater—

purposes that would bring myself and others into the more abundant life God desires for all of us.

As I relive these memories, I can clearly see how many times the Enemy tried to cripple my obedience with the original deception. Whenever I became frustrated, the Enemy would be right there to plant doubts about God's character in my mind. "Why is it that every time you find something you think is fun, God asks you to lay it down? Why is He being so strict and harsh with you? None of these things are a big deal at all." Satan was always trying to make me distrust the Lord's intentions for me.

Of course all of the Enemy's whispers were lies. God wasn't asking me to lay down *everything* I enjoyed in life. There were other hobbies I enjoyed during that time, like playing basketball and working out, and I felt God's peace to engage in them. And even when I was being asked to lay something down, it was only because God's plan for my future was infinitely better—a truth I see clearly now.

> **The Lord spoke clearly to my heart and said, "She is not the one for you."**

Waiting for the One

Not long after I started college, I met a girl and we began dating. We were extremely compatible—we both loved the Lord, we went to the same church, and we were close with each other's families. On the surface, everything seemed perfect. As I approached the end of college, our relationship became more serious, and most everyone assumed we would get married.

> **That moment of obedience**
> **proved a fork in the road**
> **for me—a time when I left**
> **camp and began to climb**
> **higher up the mountain.**

Yet as much as I cared for this person, I felt some uncertainty in my heart about whether she was the one I was supposed to marry. The confusing part was that there seemed to be many more positives than negatives to our relationship. Still, these feelings continued to grow in my heart, and as they did I tried to ignore what I sensed the Lord was telling me because I really cared about her—and I knew that breaking up would be very painful for both of us.

Finally, one morning as I was praying about it, the Lord spoke clearly to my heart and said, "She is not the one for you." The finality of these words was so intense it was as if the Lord had branded them into the depths of my soul. Instead of obeying I told the Lord, "I won't do it. I won't break up with her." I realize now I had two motivations: First, I genuinely cared about her. But second, I knew she thought highly of me and selfishly I didn't want to do anything to tarnish my image in her eyes.

I resisted the Lord on this issue for several months. During that time, our relationship took a turn for the worse and it was completely my fault. I should have been obedient immediately, but I wasn't. As God's conviction grew stronger, my heart began to move away from her. As my feelings changed I struggled to cherish her the way she deserved. Part of the motivation for my resisting the Lord was to preserve her from pain. As it turned out my hesitancy to obey was hurting her more than if I had immediately ended the relationship—I was stringing her along and compounding the pain.

Eventually, I could no longer resist my conviction from the Lord. I ended our relationship, and unlike the video game situation, there was no instant relief. She did not understand and her family did not understand. They questioned whether I was really hearing from God. The whole situation was extremely painful for everyone involved.

Following the breakup, it was like the floodgates opened in my life and one thing after another began to fall apart. The months that followed became one of the toughest seasons of my life. I questioned God as to why, when I obeyed Him, the situation seemed to get harder instead of easier. Again, the original deception was lurking in my heart, trying to get me to lean on my own understanding and doubt God's good intentions.

Now, many years later, it is easy to see the goodness God was trying to bring into my life. Through the dark season that followed, God taught me some of the greatest lessons of my life and built character in me that has proved priceless over the years.

That moment of obedience proved a fork in the road for me—a time when I left camp and began to climb higher up the mountain.

My whole life was focused on the goal of making sure I would always be liked and accepted.

It was also not long after that when God called me to go and work for the youth ministry I mentioned at the beginning of the chapter. My time there was one of the most formative experiences of my life and laid the foundation for what I am doing today. But looking back, I really don't think I would have made the decision to go if I had been engaged. And even if I did go, having a family would have made it impossible for me to throw my life into my tasks at work the way I did. I also wouldn't have been able to spend months away from home on the mission field. I cannot imagine what my life would be like without these experiences. I also look at the marriage God has given me today and I shudder to think about missing out on the person I have come to realize was the one God had in store for me all along.

It wasn't just my life in which God was working for good, either. She too went on to get married, and the last I heard she has a great marriage and family. God was working good for all involved.

Again, we see that God's intentions are *always* for our benefit. He is *always* looking to lead us to a more abundant life.

Even if we can't see how things will work out for good right now, we can trust that one day we will have the perspective to appreciate God's leading. From the top of the mountain, the painful experiences of our lives become glowing testimonies of God's gracious guidance.

Overcoming Insecurity

Because of my childhood, my insecurities were one of the hardest things I have ever had to surrender. You may remember me talking about some of the rejection I endured in elementary school. Through these and other events in my life, by the time I entered high school, insecurity controlled me like a puppeteer manipulating a puppet. However, when I became popular in high school, I no longer had to face much rejection. I mistook this to mean that my insecurities had been resolved. On the contrary, my insecurities hadn't gone away at all—they simply sank below the surface where I was less aware of how they were navigating the controls of my life.

Not long after I graduated from college and began working for the youth ministry, God began to slowly deal with my insecurity. I was twenty-three years old when the Lord spoke to me and said, "Mike, your entire personality is nothing but a defense mechanism that you have developed so you will never have to face rejection again." What He showed me was that my whole life was focused on the goal of making sure I would always be liked and accepted. I remember having a little midlife crisis at twenty-three and thinking: *If what I know myself to be now is nothing more than a defense mechanism, then who am I?*

About this time God began to open doors for me to speak

publicly. He had already begun taking me through the process of facing my insecurities in several areas, and it wasn't comfortable! Speaking in public just added more fuel to the refiner's fire. What if I didn't do a good job, or people didn't like what I had to say? Knowing that I ultimately felt called to speak only added to the pressure I felt to succeed.

In my early days of speaking, due to my insecurities, I would only accept about one invitation a month. I felt like I needed to practically memorize my sermon so I could deliver it perfectly. And if I didn't get tons of positive feedback at the end of the message, Satan was right there to breathe life into my fears that I had failed. The whole process was extremely stressful.

I remember the Lord gave me an example. He said, "Mike, you are like a fine china plate. Just like china only comes out on the finest of occasions, you only want to be used if everything is going to go perfectly." But He reminded me that china doesn't get used very often. Then He said, "Mike, I want to convert you to a Wal-Mart plate. Then I can use you all the time regardless of the occasion." The point came across loud and clear—my insecurities were preventing God from using me the way He desired.

Over the next several years, the Lord continued to challenge me in the area of my insecurity. He often gave me opportunities to face and overcome my fears, and I experienced a measure of progress. That was when God determined I was ready, and He took me through a situation that went straight to the heart of my lifelong insecurity.

When I turned twenty-six, my hair started to fall out. For many people this would not be a big deal, but for me it felt like the end of the world. I had spent my whole life trying to build an image that was rejection-proof. In my mind, being bald was going to ruin everything I had spent my whole life building. *I'll probably be a lot less popular because I'm going to look like an idiot,* I told myself. *Girls won't find me attractive anymore, so I'll probably never get married. This could ruin my entire future in ministry, because who will want to hear some ugly bald guy preach?*

These fears may sound absurd to you, but they were very real to me. I wrestled with thoughts like these all the time. That's what happens when you have a deception like insecurity. I had believed lies from the Enemy for so long that they seemed like the truth to me.

"You have served your image your entire life. You choose this day whom you will serve."

It all started the day I met with a friend I hadn't seen in several years. As we were catching up, he innocently mentioned that my hair was thinning. I kindly told him that he was mistaken and my hair was just naturally very fine and was not thinning at all.

When I returned home, I examined myself in the mirror and realized that he was right. I panicked. I spent the next day or so researching the latest, greatest lotions and potions that were guaranteed to make my balding head grow hair like a Chia Pet. I finally settled on a $300 kit—my image was worth any price. I even paid extra for overnight shipping.

When it finally arrived, I couldn't wait to rip into the package and get started "fixing" my problem. Just as I was about to open the package, I felt the Lord speak to my heart and say, "Send it back."

My composed response was something like: *What?!*

He said it again. "Send it back." Then He said, "Mike, you have served your image your entire life. You choose this day whom you will serve." He instructed me to do nothing to alter the process because He was going to use it in my life.

Obviously, the best response would have been to be like Abraham when God spoke to him about sacrificing his son, Isaac. The Bible says that he got up early the next morning and immediately obeyed God. But I figured it would be much more spiritual to pray about it for the next three days. So that's exactly what I did. For the next three days I begged God to change His mind and not make me go through with this. I remember Him speaking to me and saying, "Mike, because I love you, if this is not necessary, I won't ask you to go through it. But if I do, it will only be because it will be so beneficial to your life that it will be worth the pain. Either way, you win."

As you can tell by looking at my picture on this book, the Lord did not change His mind, and I sent my hair-growth kit back. Over the next several years, the Lord asked me to face my fears and insecurities head-on (pun intended). No longer could I avoid facing situations where I might feel rejection— no matter how well I prepared my talk, I still had to accept that I didn't look like I thought I should look. Every time I looked in the mirror, I was reminded that there was a flaw in my image and that I was vulnerable to rejection.

It is an understatement to say that this process shook me to the core of my identity. The Enemy works differently with all of us and your struggles may be different. But for me, the acceptance of others was the core issue in my life. Everything I had believed about where my value came from as a person was built on a lie.

As I followed Jesus in obedience, He patiently helped me walk through each fear and expose each lie. With every step of surrender, insecurity's power over me was lessened and I began to walk in a freedom I had never known. I had to reprogram my mind by replacing Satan's lies with God's truth. God showed me that my security is found in Him. I learned that my value in God's eyes never changes. He loves me perfectly, and His opinion is the only one that matters.

If I had not surrendered in this area, I'm sure I would still be a Christian and I would probably be serving God in some capacity. But I can promise you my life would not match God's design—I would be camped out far down the mountain, with my insecurities weighing me down and preventing me from climbing higher. The Enemy had built a wall of fear across the road to my destiny. God called me to boldly proclaim His truth regardless of the response, and insecurity was preventing me from accomplishing my purpose. Only by allowing God to lead me to freedom in this area could His amazing plans come to pass in my life.

There are so many other examples of God's goodness that came through my surrender in this area. One in particular that always amazed me was with my wife, Alicia. I met her right in the middle of this process. She was this beautiful, amazing girl that almost every guy seemed to be interested in—and she was interested in me! At one point we were having a conversation and I asked her if it ever bothered her that I was losing my hair. I'll never forget her response: "No way! This probably will sound weird to you, but I have always been attracted to guys with no hair. Even if you had more hair, I would like it better shaved."

Every time God speaks to you, it is a fork in the road in your life.

One of the main lies the Enemy would use to try to get me to turn back from following Jesus' lead was that losing my hair would hurt my chances of finding a girl. If I had leaned on my own understanding and not surrendered, I may have made myself more attractive in the eyes of most other girls, but I would have been less attractive to the only girl whose opinion mattered. Isn't it great to know that God knows what He's doing, and that He always—*always*—has our best interest in mind?

The Choice Is Yours

I want to be clear that my stories are not formulas that can be applied to everyone. For example, there is nothing inherently wrong with fantasy football, video games, investments . . . or hair, for that matter. What I hope you see is that each person's walk with God needs to be a Spirit-led walk

(Galatians 5:25). We all have the Bible, but God has also sent us the Holy Spirit to speak to each person about how God would have us respond in every situation. God shapes each person differently according to the plan He has for them. Some choices may generate an area of struggle for you but not for your neighbor, and vice versa. No matter what another Christian is doing, each of us is accountable to respond to the leading of the Spirit in our own lives. Don't reject the conviction of the Lord because He does not seem to be convicting your neighbor about the same issue.

Every time God speaks to you, it is a fork in the road in your life. If you ignore Him, you will miss out on some of the great things He has planned for you. However, if you surrender to Him when He speaks to you, you will immediately begin to experience God in new and exciting ways.

I truly believe that God has given you this book to remind you that He loves you so much and that He wants you to trust Him. God's hope is that you will start surrendering to Him immediately so that He can pour out His goodness into your life.

How you respond is up to you. Will you continue on the path you are on? Or will you let Jesus be Lord of your entire life and follow Him up to the mountaintop? It may not be an easy path, and it may be more comfortable to remain at the base camp, but it is the only path that leads to experiencing all that God has for you.

I have walked both paths. I have resisted the Lord's instruction, and I have responded with surrender, and I can promise you: There is no comparison.

Questions

1. In what ways have you noticed life being like a minefield?

2. Which story of surrender spoke to you the most? Why?

3. Do you sense any areas of your life where God may be speaking to you about a greater level of surrender to Him?

4. On a scale of one to ten, with one being the least and ten being the most, how much peace are you feeling right now? If you answered on the lower end of the scale, what do you think is causing your peace to be disturbed?

5. What are some ways you can prepare yourself so that when God instructs you, you will resist leaning on your own understanding and trust God instead?

chapter 10

all in?

As our journey together through this book comes to an end, the rest of your journey is beginning. God is calling you to the summit of the mountain where the fullness of His abundant life is waiting, and you must choose how you will respond. The choice is simple: *camp* or *climb*. Choosing to climb—to go all in—requires a decision to make Jesus Lord of all. You may have already made a decision to invite Jesus into your heart, but this is something more. Jesus is not looking for an invitation to your heart. He is looking for ownership of your heart.

Think about the difference between these two scenarios. If you own a house and invite someone over, you still make the rules and call the shots. But if you sign the deed of ownership of your house over to someone else, it's an entirely different story—now they're in charge. It's not your house anymore; it belongs to them.

Jesus is not looking for an invitation to your heart. He is looking for ownership of your heart.

This is the kind of relationship God is looking for with you. If Jesus is merely an invited guest in your life, you're still in control, and you'll never experience the radical transformation He promises. Such transformation and blessing only occur when Jesus *owns* your life.

Total Surrender

Mark chapter 10 illustrates this principle perfectly. It tells the story of a rich young man who comes to Jesus because he realizes that something is missing in his life. When he finds Jesus, he falls at Jesus' feet and asks Him what is missing. Jesus had not yet gone to the cross, so He directs Him back to the law and tells him to follow the commandments. He responds to Jesus that he has been doing all those things since he was a child but still something is missing.

When I read this it paints a perfect portrait of many of our lives today. This guy would clearly be someone who today would call himself a Christian. He had probably been going to church his whole life and was doing his best to follow the things he learned there. But he knew that there had to be more.

At that point Jesus looked at him with love and issued

him the very invitation we have been discussing in this book—
the invitation to make Him Lord of all.

"One thing you lack," Jesus said. "Go, sell everything you
have and give to the poor, and you will have treasure in heaven.
Then come, follow me" (Mark 10:21).

Jesus is pointing out to this young man that he is with-
holding something from God's control—his riches. The young
man was willing to make Jesus Lord of every area *except* that
one. However, we simply cannot follow Jesus if He is not the
number one priority in our lives. Jesus tells him to get rid of
that idol *so that he will be completely surrendered.*

Jesus encourages him that parting with his idol will be
well worth the sacrifice—remember that Jesus longs to bless
us and lead us into abundant life. Unfortunately, the young
man decides—at least for the moment—that the price is too
great. He is not willing to allow Jesus to be Lord of that area
of his life. Apparently, he was passionate about inviting Jesus
into his life, but he wasn't quite ready to give Him ownership.
The Bible records that he walked away sorrowful, and we
never hear about him again. What a missed opportunity to
follow Christ!

**God asks us for complete
and total surrender.**

Meanwhile, the disciples were watching this whole encounter happen. After the rich young man walked away, they
approached Jesus and said something like, "Jesus, what about

us? I mean, that guy may not have been willing to follow You, but we have already left everything to follow You." Jesus responds with an amazing promise: "I tell you the truth, . . . no one who has left home or brothers or sisters or mother or father or children or fields for me and the gospel will fail to receive a hundred times as much in this present age (homes, brothers, sisters, mothers, children and fields—and with them, persecutions) and in the age to come, eternal life" (Mark 10:29–30).

The difference between holding back one thing and giving up everything is the difference between experiencing sorrow or blessing. God asks us for complete and total surrender. *Anything* short of that leads to a minimal and unfulfilling experience with God.

The Great Divide

This decision is the great divide between those who experience God and those who do not, and making the choice to surrender all to Jesus is how we cross over. The majority of people choose to stay on the side of the great divide where God is rarely experienced. Their insistence on holding back from the Lord keeps them on the side of lesser experience—like the rich young man. But those who choose to hold nothing back cross over to the side where God is greatly experienced— like the disciples. The key to abundant life is found in choosing to step over that point of no return—to surrender everything—because it is on the other side of the great divide that our lives are transformed and blessed.

Please understand that truly experiencing God does *not* mean we need to be perfect. God is not looking for perfection—He is looking for *surrender*. Perfection means we never fail, but surrender means we are always willing to remain yielded to Jesus *even when we fail.* God's call is for us to maintain a stance of surrender in every area of our lives. No one can be perfect, but everyone must determine where they stand on God's call to surrender everything.

Just like the rich young man, you are now faced with that choice. Will you put down this book and walk away sorrowful, knowing that you are not willing to let Jesus take total control of your life? Or will you choose to surrender everything and follow Him? Your life has now reached the edge of the great divide and you must choose how you will respond.

Going All In

I want you to consider joining me in prayer to ask God to take complete ownership of your life. Please don't go through the motions because it seems like the "right" thing to do. This prayer is between you and God alone, and God knows your heart. Going through the motions won't change anything. But if the prayer in the next section expresses the desire of your heart, God will honor it.

Don't make your decision based on whether you feel you are *able* to obey God in every area. God will give you the strength as He transforms you into a new person. The question is, Are you *willing* to give Him control and begin following His lead each day? A willing heart is what God is looking for.

If, after reading the prayer, you are not sure you're ready to make that kind of commitment, or you need some time to think about it, I would encourage you to think about it for a few days or longer if you need to. Consider what it will really be like to reorganize your life around yielding to God in every area. What would that look like for you? What things in your life may need to change? If after further consideration you are ready, then come back to the prayer and pray it at that time.

If you feel that you are not willing to make this commitment right now and you want to skip over it and continue reading, that's okay—really. God wants our honest surrender, not lip service. Perhaps you can start by asking God to change your heart and bring you to the place where you are ready to give Him everything. As He works in your life, you may become ready and can make the commitment at that time.

God promises that *as you follow through* with that commitment every day, your life will drastically change.

After you have considered your decision carefully, if you are ready to continue, I want you to think of this moment like a wedding. You are at the altar, so to speak, making a lifelong vow of commitment to the Lord. When you're ready, take some time to commit the following prayer to the Lord.

"Jesus, today I bring You my life, and I surrender every area of it to Your Lordship. I invite You not just to come into my life but to have ownership of it. I know there will be many times of great joy as I follow You. And I also know that at times following You will be difficult. I realize that there will be times You may instruct me in ways I don't understand, to protect me from dangers I can't see. Help me trust You when those times come. Give me the strength to choose You when you lead me in ways that are different from what I desire. Help me to trust in Your goodness and love for me. I know I won't be perfect, Jesus, but I promise to never quit. On this day I pledge to follow You for better or for worse in my life. Now I ask You, will you lead me? Will you help me hear Your voice so I can know what You have called me to do? I thank You for Your salvation, and I look forward to walking through this life with You and seeing You face-to-face when I am done. Jesus, from this day forward, I am Yours completely. In Jesus' name I pray, amen!"

Now take a few minutes to express your heart to the Lord in your own words.

At this moment you may be feeling some serious fireworks going off in your heart, or you may just be feeling a quiet determination, but whether you feel anything or not, a spiritual line has been crossed in your heart. You have finally responded to God in exactly the way He called you. God promises that *as you follow through* with that commitment every day, your life will drastically change. You are going to begin experiencing God like never before. Over time you are going to watch His promises come to pass in your life. People around you will start to notice the change that Jesus is making in you. You are in for the journey of a lifetime. Congratulations! You have just gone all in.

What Now?

The moment you choose to give everything you are to Christ, your journey has just begun. Taking this step is like leaving base camp. While others choose to remain camped on the slopes, you have joined the few who decide to journey to the summit. By living out that decision each day and following Jesus, you will climb higher and experience more of God.

Now that you are committed to your journey, you may be wondering, "What do I do now? How do I begin to actually live out a life that is fully surrendered to Christ?" Each day we must be willing to do some very practical things. We need to seek God so we can hear His instructions—and then we need to obey them as we continue to move forward.

Hearing from God

The term "following Jesus" implies that He is leading us. One of the first things we must do if we are going to walk with God is learn how to hear His voice.

Sometimes people will say, "God doesn't speak to me." Don't buy into that lie of the Enemy. John 10:27 says plainly, "My sheep hear My voice" (NASB). God *will* speak to you—He speaks to all His children.

God is speaking to us all the time, but we need to learn how to listen and recognize His voice. Many times we miss His speaking to us because we are looking for some profound experience—a vision or a voice from heaven. The reality is that most of the time God speaks to us in very simple ways.

For example, every time we read the Bible and understand something, God is speaking to us. It is comforting to know that we can hear God speak anytime simply by reading the Bible. God's Word is full of stories, instructions, poems, prayers, and wisdom—and *all* of it is God speaking to us and helping us to live better lives! We can read the Bible straight through or search out specific Scriptures on a topic we are struggling with. If we are going to be serious about following Him, we have to dedicate time to reading Scripture. Our goal in reading the Bible is not just to learn—it is also to *apply* what we learn. Set some goals to spend time in God's Word every day.

God can also speak to us through prayer. If we dedicate time to prayer, not only will we begin to see God answer our prayers, but we will learn to hear His voice. Prayer is a conversation with God where we talk to Him and He talks to us. When we first start listening for God's voice in prayer, there may be some trial and error involved. God speaks to us through our thoughts, and sometimes it can be hard to determine which thoughts are God speaking and which are not. Over time this will become clear.

If we take the time to listen, we will surely hear His voice.

There are countless other ways God can speak. He can speak through a song or a sermon at church. He can speak through a friend or parent. He can speak through nature or the circumstances of life.

The key is to be willing and ready to hear from God—and then to build into your life opportunities for that to happen.

Read your Bible, listen to a worship song on your iPod, or take a hike in silence. Pray with a friend. Memorize a verse.

God is always speaking to us because He is eager to reveal His perfect will to us. If we take the time to listen, we will surely hear His voice.

Obeying His Voice

When we hear God's voice, we quickly discover certain things that we need to start doing and other things that we need to stop doing. If we want to continue to grow, we must obey His instructions. We can *hear* God's voice all day long, but if we don't *do* what He tells us, we won't experience Him. However, if we form habits in our life of listening and obeying, our level of experience with God will be off the charts!

Begin right now by taking a quick inventory of what you feel God is speaking to you. Perhaps there have been things you have felt convicted to do or stop doing as you've been reading this book. That is God speaking to you! Take some time immediately to think through how you can take some steps of obedience in those areas—and then do them. Too often we complicate our walk with God by procrastinating or trying to figure out why God is asking something instead of simply obeying. This will almost always just lead to confusion and missed opportunities. It doesn't matter whether the instruction is big or small, or even whether we understand it in the moment. The way to keep growing is to keep obeying God when He speaks to us.

If we continually obey, we will never stop making progress up the mountain and experiencing more of God.

Keep Moving Forward

So much of success in following Jesus comes from the mindset to keep moving forward. Too many times I see people who go back to camping out because they failed a few times and started believing they just couldn't do it. Everyone fails at times. But if we simply never quit, eventually we will overcome (Galatians 6:9).

I cannot tell you how many times I have started out by failing miserably when God convicted me in an area. It seemed if I were given ten opportunities in a day to obey in that area, I would fail them all. Then after much work, I might succeed two or three out of ten times. I thought I would never overcome. But I have found that if I will just hang in there and not settle or justify my sin, eventually God will lead me to victory. Pretty soon I would pass five or six out of ten. Then it was eight or nine. Eventually, I would find that God had given me complete victory and it was no longer an area of struggle in my life. If you will learn to keep moving forward, even in the face of failure, you will eventually be victorious and continue to climb the mountain.

Proverbs 24:16 says, "Though a righteous man falls seven times, he rises again." This man isn't righteous because he never falls. The verse says he falls, seven times. What makes him righteous is that each time he falls, he rises again. This is the difference between perfection and surrender. God doesn't expect us never to fall, but He does expect us to get right back up and keep moving forward!

Determine in your mind to keep following Jesus no matter what. Some days you may feel like you fail every time you turn around. That's okay. Repent, get back up, and keep moving forward—the view from the top of the mountain will be well worth the struggle!

Final Thoughts

When you choose to go all in and take the necessary steps each day to live in surrender, you *will* experience God. But there is one final benefit. As you allow God to transform you, your life will inspire others to go all in as well. When your friends and family see the level of your experience with God, and the real transformation in your life, they will want to have what you have. My sincere prayer for you is that your life will be so radically transformed that it will cause many others to rise up and begin to climb to the peak of all that God has for them.

History proves that when enough people within a generation grab hold of their destiny and begin forsaking all to follow Christ, revolutions happen. We have seen this prove true in certain generations of Israelites throughout the Old Testament. We saw it in the generation of the first believers in Jesus' day. We have seen it in America during the great awakenings. We have witnessed these revolutions take place in other nations as great revivals have broken out at different times. Perhaps as we press on toward the peak, others will be inspired to follow . . . and then others will follow them. And then, perhaps God will bring a revolution in our day that future generations will speak of. History proves that when we give our all to Him, He will always respond and glorify His name. As for me, I am going to keep climbing and inspire as many as I can to do the same. See you at the top!

Questions

1. Did you pray the prayer of commitment in the chapter? Why or why not?

2. Are there any areas of your life you already feel the Lord speaking to you about? What is He saying? Are you willing to follow His leading in that area? Why or why not?

3. What has been your experience hearing from God to this point in your life?

4. What steps can you take so that you hear from God more?

5. What daily steps are you prepared to take in order to ensure that you will continue growing in your relationship and experience with God?

acknowledgments

My mother-in-law, Kea Waldon–Thank you for all of your advice on the manuscript and, of course, all your help babysitting so I could write.

My parents, Jim and Linda Stump–Thank you for raising me and for your example and encouragement to pursue the Lord. Dad, thank you for all your time and effort helping me edit the original manuscript.

Don and Jenni and D. C. Jacobson & Associates–Thank you for all of your time and insight. I couldn't imagine doing this without your help.

My daughter, Bella–Thank you for bringing such joy to my life and putting a smile on my face every time I needed one.

My wife, Alicia–Thank you for your love and support. They mean more than I could describe with words. Your advice and recently discovered editing skills have been invaluable in creating this book. I love you!

My Savior Jesus—Thank You for Your incomprehensible love that continues to draw my heart all in.

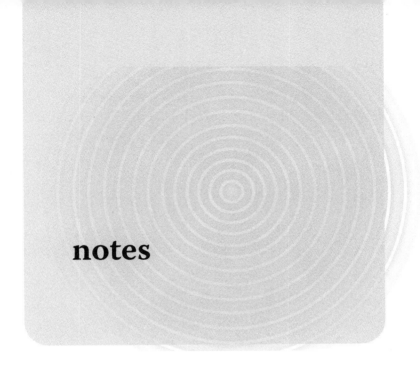

notes

Introduction

1. Quoted in Philip Yancey, *What's So Amazing about Grace?* (Grand Rapids: Zondervan, 2002), 13–14.

Chapter 1: Camping Out or Climbing?

1. "Faith Has a Limited Effect On Most People's Behavior," Barna Group, http://www.barna.org/barna-update/article/5-barna-update/188-faith-has-a-limited-effect-on-most-peoples-behavior.

2. As revealed in a 2002 report from the Southern Baptist Convention's Council on Family Life, summarized at http://www.sbcannualmeeting.net/sbc02/newsroom/newspage.asp?ID=261.

3. From *Thayer's Greek Lexicon*, Electronic Database, © 2002, 2003, 2006 by Biblesoft, Inc. All rights reserved.

Chapter 2

1. If you struggle with severe depression or suicidal thoughts it is an important step to seek godly and/or professional counsel.

For more information visit:

WWW.MIKEGUZZARDO.ORG

For booking inquiries: contact@mikeguzzardo.org
Follow Mike!
Twitter: @MikeGuzzardo1
Facebook: Mike Guzzardo

MOODY
PUBLISHERS
www.MoodyPublishers.com

MORE TITLES FROM ...

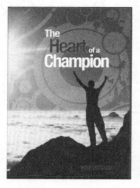

THE HEART OF A CHAMPION

"For the eyes of the Lord range throughout the earth to strengthen those whose hearts are fully committed to Him . . ." (2 Chronicles 16:9). This verse tells us that God is constantly searching back and forth across the earth, looking for people to engage in His mission. When He finds the right person, He will strengthen or literally show Himself strong on their behalf. This is good news, but what type of person is He looking for? He is looking for a heart that is fully committed to Him—the heart of a champion. This powerful six-CD series will unveil how to develop the kind of heart that stops the very eyes of God as they search the earth and then moves Him to show Himself strong in accomplishing His destiny through you.

LOVE SERIES

Jesus was once asked, "Of all the commandments, which is the most important?" He answered that loving God and loving others was most important of all. Learning to receive God's love and then give it to others is life's utmost mission. God's desire is for us to be so transformed by His love that it pours through us to others. This five-CD series explores topics such as grasping God's love, loving yourself, loving others, sex and relationships, and the ultimate act of love.

MOODY
PUBLISHERS

www.MoodyPublishers.com

... Mike Guzzardo

What the Devil Hopes You Never Find Out About Yourself

This CD will dispel some of the traps of the enemy that keep us from discovering who we are in Christ—traps like comparison, succumbing to other people's opinions, and being deceived by false beliefs about ourselves.

Sex and Relationships

Mike outlines the dangers of stepping outside God's plan for love, gives specifics about how to walk in a godly relationship with the opposite sex, and then shares from his own journey in this area.

Intimacy with God

Every area of our lives is illuminated when we walk in intimacy with God. Whether we seek direction, peace, joy, fulfillment, or transformation, intimacy with God is the answer. Mike also discusses many of the common battlefields where intimacy will be won or lost on a daily basis in our lives.

MOODY
PUBLISHERS

www.MoodyPublishers.com

THE COFFEE HOUSE CHRONICLES

ISBN: 978-0-8024-8768-1

ISBN: 978-0-8024-8766-7

ISBN: 978-0-8024-8767-4

Also available as EBooks:

ISBN: 978-1-57567-940-2

ISBN: 978-1-57567-938-9

ISBN: 978-1-57567-939-6

With over 40 million books sold, bestselling author Josh McDowell is no stranger to creatively presenting biblical truth. Now, partnering with fellow apologist Dave Sterrett, Josh introduces a new series targeted at the intersection of story and truth.

The Coffee House Chronicles are short, easily devoured novellas aimed at answering prevalent spiritual questions. Each book in the series tackles a long-contested question of the faith, and then answers these questions with truth through relationships and dialogue in each story.

MOODY
PUBLISHERS

www.MoodyPublishers.com

THE BARE FACTS

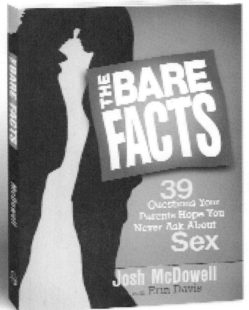

ISBN: 978-0-8024-0255-4

Also available as an EBook 978-0-8024-7838-2

*Sex is everywhere. And misunderstandings about it are even more
pervasive. Whether you have questions of your own and don't know who to
ask, or you are being asked questions and don't know where to turn—this
small book has the answers. Bestselling author and speaker Josh McDowell
believes that no question is off-limits and that knowledge, not ignorance, is
the key to youthful purity and a fulfilling marriage and family. This book
builds on that approach with relevant, pertinent statistics, entertaining
anecdotes, and real stories.*

MOODY
PUBLISHERS
www.MoodyPublishers.com